P9-DFO-928

BEFORE YOU CAN DISCIPLINE...

Vital Professional Foundations For Classroom Management

BY
Robert L. DeBruyn

The Master Teacher, Inc.
Publisher
Manhattan, Kansas
U.S.A.

THE MASTER TEACHER, INC.
Publisher
Leadership Lane
P.O. Box 1207
Manhattan, Kansas 66502

Library of Congress Catalog Card Number: 83-62446
ISBN 0-914607-03-0
First Printing 1983
Second Printing 1985
Printed in the United States of America

Dedicated to giving teachers less problem time and more teaching time.

— ROBERT L. DeBRUYN

TABLE OF CONTENTS

Chapter Four
STRATEGIC ACTION

INTRODUCTION

The place of discipline in our schools continues to be a number one priority. A look at any poll — Phi Delta Kappa, Gallup, National Education Association, or local newspaper survey — reveals that discipline is seen by educators and parents alike as the number one problem at home as well as at school. It's easy to see why.

We are professionals trained to teach academic subjects and our training is extensive. Unfortunately, we are not trained extensively to understand and implement usable professional and personal strategic attitudes, positions, and actions which are effective in getting a child who is not behaving in acceptable ways to do so, so that we can teach — and a class full of children can learn.

Because we have thirty or more students in class and a wide variety of things to do each day, it's not always easy to come up with one technique to manage a misbehaving student. And it's not just the habitual discipline problem we have to worry about. It's the countless different misbehaviors we see in kids who normally behave that we must manage effectively. There are talking in class, tardiness, disrespect, complaining, fighting, troublemaking, defying, and many, many more behaviors that we must deal with repeatedly. That's why this book was written. It is a *foundation* book for learning how to look at behavior, develop a professional strategic attitude, adopt a professional strategic position, and take a professional strategic action. This book was written in conjunction with, and as a prelude to, *You Can Handle Them All — A Discipline Model for Handling Over One Hundred Different Misbehaviors at Home and at School.* It should be read prior to using this practical guide for relating to *specific* student behaviors.

Foundations are vitally important in learning to be a good, caring, and effective disciplinarian. An important part of discipline is professional understanding of the teacher's role in discipline situations. To be effective, a teacher must first adopt specific professional attitudes. Second, a teacher must understand the predictable behavior which results from individual student needs. Third, a teacher must take a strategic professional position which facilitates success. Finally, a teacher must acquire a wide assortment of skills for treating the problem behavior.

In order for us to communicate effectively, however, we need a working definition of discipline. Therefore, I ask that you accept and use the following simple definition: Discipline is the adjustment of unacceptable behavior to acceptable behavior. In addition, I ask that you accept the fact that at least three specifics support this definition:

1. Our teaching must promote self-discipline. We tell students over and over to do certain things. However, our attitude, position, and action for discipline in our classrooms should be designed to help children learn to do what they are supposed to do on their own.

2. Students must know what the standards are in our classrooms. Persuasive communication with students is a must. There are too many natural rule and regulation variations within a class and a school for discipline to be learned without student-teacher communication. Too many times rules change day by day, and from class to class. Too often we think students know what we expect of them without our ever telling them. We have to remember too that *standards vary* from teacher to teacher and from class to class. In truth, the standards are not the same in any two classrooms.

3. The adjustment of student behavior must fit the occasion and the environment. Behavior standards change — from the classroom, to the auditorium, to the halls, to the cafeteria. Children will — and should — act differently in each of these environments. Students can run in the gym. They can talk in the cafeteria. Therefore, our behavioral expectations must be adjustable rather than rigid, depending on the situation and the environment.

With this definition of discipline in mind, along with these three specific teaching conditions, you are ready to read this book. It is intended to be a professional foundation for managing the behavior of students — as well as your own.

CHAPTER 1

STUDENT NEEDS INFLUENCE APPROPRIATE AND INAPPROPRIATE BEHAVIOR

PART ONE

EVERY DISCIPLINE PROBLEM HAS THREE VARIABLES

Rationale: There are three variables in every discipline situation: the misbehaving student, the class, and the teacher. Unless a teacher can control his or her own behavior, all three factors remain variables — and chaos is the predictable result.

If we could somehow remove the discipline problem from the school scene, our contentment, satisfaction, and happiness in teaching might rise appreciably in an instant. Certainly, much of the frustration and despair we experience as teachers would disappear. The resulting state of mind would probably make us all better teachers immediately. But discipline problems will always exist. However, they can be minimized. They can be managed quickly and effectively. That's why it's important and necessary that we continually upgrade and improve our ability to cope with them in a professional and successful way.

Understanding Affects Our Strategic Approach

In discipline situations, teacher approach and attitude are paramount. Many teachers think a misbehaving student should admit wrongdoing immediately, apologize, and never demonstrate that particular behavior again.

Even if this is not what we think, our behavior and action in discipline situations would tend to make one believe it to be. Too often our thinking is totally in terms of student adjustment. Seldom do we think predominantly in terms of teacher adjustment. We should, because failing to do so is our first mistake in handling discipline problems.

To be an effective disciplinarian, the teacher must become the primary adjustor. That's a fact. A teacher can be successful in getting students to adjust their behavior only by first adjusting his or her own. It's through teacher adjustment that we are enabled to employ various methods, techniques, and skills necessary to get students to change their behavior — and manage a class in the process.

We all know teachers who never make any adjustments. Rather, they look to the student to be the sole adjustor. In addition, many think only of handling discipline problems with a three-step approach. First, they try to be nice. Second, if they don't find success in being nice, they think in terms of being mean. Finally, if being nice or being mean doesn't work, they think in terms of asking their administrator to get the student out of the classroom. A teacher's repertoire of human relations skills needs to be greater than three techniques if he or she is to be effective in handling discipline problems. That's why it's absolutely imperative that we understand the variables which exist in *all* discipline situations.

The Three Variables And You

Every classroom discipline problem has at least three variables: the teacher, the problem student, and the rest of the class. All these variables are interrelated and affect each other — in both the present and future senses. Equally important, each remains a variable until teacher adjustment makes it controllable. Teachers would be wise to ponder this simple but profound fact, for it is vital to their effectiveness.

If you will think about it for a moment, common sense will reveal that there is only one of the three variables that a teacher can always control immediately; that variable is himself or herself. If a teacher cannot control his or her own behavior in a discipline situation, he or she will only increase the probability of more trouble with the other two variables — not just the misbehaving student. In truth, herein lies a basic problem of most teachers who fail in discipline situations. Their response to misbehavior is personal rather than professional. Worse, they think in terms of student adjustment rather than teacher adjustment.

For example, if a doctor told me to lose twenty pounds and, when I returned for an examination, found that I had not lost weight, what should the doctor do? Should he or she rant, rave, threaten, issue ultimatums, or kick me out of the office? Should he or she tell me I don't deserve medical advice? Absolutely not. His or her reaction must be professional. He or she must think in terms of professional doctor adjustment. The problem is mine — not the doctor's. I did not fail to lose weight to spite him or her. If I had, my problem would be magnified. Regardless, only by relating to me professionally, and adjusting methods and techniques in procedure, can the doctor hope to help me solve my problem. That's the difference between reacting personally and reacting professionally. The same is true in the classroom.

If a problem arises — even if it's the umpteenth time — and the teacher explodes, what is the result? The problem has been made worse. All three variables remain, and the one which should be controlled first, the professional teacher, appears to be the one most out of control. Then, should the problem student or classmates be the ones who should be expected to balance the situation? Remember, if the teacher reacts as a controlled variable, then chances are the rest of the class will automatically become a controlled variable too. That leaves only the discipline problem to deal with rather than an entire class. That's why the teacher must be the first and primary adjustor with a discipline problem. It all begins with the teacher. No matter what the classroom incident, nothing can happen and nothing will happen in a positive way until the teacher has control of self. The vast majority of teachers who fail in discipline situations do so because they were never taught this one simple foundation principle. Even after years in the classroom, they still think it is the student, not they, who should do the adjusting.

Remember, there are three variables present in every discipline situation. The first controllable variable is you.

Those teachers with the most unsolvable discipline problems are usually those who cannot control themselves. As a result, they make every situation worse — for themselves, the problem student, and the rest of the class. Nine times out of ten their problems begin because they take every classroom incident personally and react to it in a personal way. They can magnify the dropping of a book on the floor into a major event resulting in total confusion for all. They will punish an entire class for the actions of one, stop and lecture all if one is not listening, or create a new rule with every isolated incident.

If it's obvious that a doctor must react professionally, certainly one can easily see that it's an absolute necessity for a teacher to do so. While the doctor has but one patient at a time, the teacher has a roomful of students. And the doctor seldom has witnesses. He or she serves most patients behind closed doors. Relationships with other patients may be impaired by rumor, but seldom by observed fact. This is not true for the teacher. The whole class watches and is affected by our every action. If we cannot control ourselves, then certainly there is little we can do to control the other two variables —

the problem student and the class.

Summary

Never forget, there are three variables in every discipline situation: the teacher, the student, and the class. And of the three variables, there is only one that you can control immediately — you. If you cannot control yourself, it's very unlikely that you can control either the misbehaving student or the rest of the class. That's why you, as a teacher, must be the primary adjustor in *every* discipline situation. And in the process, you must act professionally rather than react personally. If you take misbehavior personally and react personally, you will become part of the problem. In time, you may become the primary problem insofar as correcting misbehavior is concerned in your classroom — or in the halls, auditorium, or cafeteria.

PART TWO

THE SEVEN PRIMARY NEEDS

Rationale: There are seven primary human needs, and until they are met, students are not likely to focus on studying, learning, and school work, or any other task relative to the classroom.

Relating to and motivating a roomful of students every day — with their different wants, needs, and abilities — is not an easy task. Yet, it is a prerequisite for successful teaching and for managing individual as well as group behavior. Before we can even begin the task, however, we must be aware of seven primary human needs. We simply can't even begin talking about managing student behavior without looking at these seven needs. That's because these needs must be met before anyone, including students, can be motivated to be self-disciplined, much less activated to study and cooperate, be respectful, and reach for academic goals.

The Primary Needs Are The First Place To Look

An awareness of these needs is vital to being a learning leader in the classroom. They apply to every student — those we reach as well as those we don't. That's important, because even if we're successful with the majority, it's our failure with the few students who are our discipline problems that causes us so much disappointment and grief. Likewise, many students who could not be called chronic discipline problems nevertheless misbehave. Yet, we must have the skill to handle their misbehavior too. Unfortunately, overlooking these primary needs is often the reason behind our failure to get kids to behave in the classroom.

These motivators, called the primary human needs, are physiological and unlearned. They are:

Hunger	Thirst
Sex	Air
Rest	Escape from pain

Elimination of waste

Make no mistake, understanding these needs is a foundation for handling behavior successfully. Ignoring these needs can cause us to overlook the first essential step in changing unacceptable behavior to acceptable behavior.

These primary needs must always be tended, checked, balanced, cared for, and fulfilled before the secondary needs can be considered. This is paramount, because it's within the secondary needs that children are motivated to behave, cooperate, work, be considerate, be prepared for the future, or excel in school. You may say, "I can't do anything about primary needs." Yes, you can — in many, many ways — simply as an aware, caring, and concerned human being. All research states explicitly that teacher action as simple as a demonstration of caring can alter the student-teacher relationship as well as the entire climate in a classroom or school.

Primary Needs One And Two: Hunger And Thirst

There are countless reasons why students come to school *hungry* — and many do. Never assume that every child who lives in a $100,000 home has a parent who gets up to prepare breakfast. Likewise, family financial problems or spending lunch money on something else may be the cause of hunger.

The biggest causes may be inadequate diet and dieting to lose weight. Millions of people in this country fail to eat adequately for a wide variety of reasons, and this fact alters their behavior. Watch children who come to school upset, or get irritable or misbehave about 10:00 a.m. Proper eating helps good behavior and learning — empty stomachs do not. And take note: If you are one of those teachers who don't eat breakfast, grab nothing but a doughnut and a soft drink, or try to make it on coffee until noon — watch yourself. *You* may be the discipline problem in your classroom. Medical problems such as diabetes, or eating something salty, can accent the *thirst* need. They can also be the reason behind motivational problems.

Primary Need Three: Sex

Sex is revealed frequently as a primary need which results in misbehavior. There are the typical boy-girl problems as well as girl-girl and boy-boy friendship problems we see every day. Also, difficulties caused by not being included in the group and being overdeveloped or underdeveloped physically are very real problems kids experience which cause unacceptable behavior. Sexual problems also arise due to how children feel about adults of the opposite sex. Likewise, a child may be in love with the teacher. These are all sexual needs. And they are basic needs which cause kids to behave well, as well as misbehave.

Primary Need Four: Air

The fact that the highest population density per square foot exists in school is a factor when it comes to the primary need of *air.* Most of us have studied the impact of the eighteen-inch personal zone and its effects upon people. Whenever large numbers of people are put together in a confined space, behavior will be altered. In the classroom or the halls, it is very difficult for a child to find space or privacy, or to be alone. Likewise, never forget that constant failure or continuous trouble with peers can make a classroom psychologically unsafe for some children. This can affect their willingness to participate, which in turn affects both behavior and learning. A privacy corner has worked well for many a teacher.

Primary Need Five: Rest

We're all aware of the human need for *rest.* Yet, we may not remember that kids may not be getting their rest because of worries, family problems, or illness, in addition to jobs and responsibilities at home. Remember, school may be a big part of a child's life, but it is not the only part. Likewise, we need to remember that the need for rest extends beyond sleep. Students also need rest from pressure and work. Therefore, depriving recess, social, and similar privileges may be counterproductive to getting good behavior and academic motivation in the classroom. Rest is a primary need that must be filled in order for students to work, play, sit, listen, read, study, and participate in all other school activities.

Primary Need Six: Escape From Pain

Fear is a big motivator. In fact, it may be one of the biggest in the lives of people, including students. A close look will reveal that an attempt to *escape from pain* is often the reason for a lack of learning motivation as well as for certain misbehavior. For instance, students may get in trouble for skipping school or talking back to a teacher, but feel that such behavior won't cause them nearly as much pain as everyone finding out they can't do class work. It's absolutely amazing what people will do — and not do — to avoid pain. And a teacher must look to this primary need at the first sign of misbehavior because school failure is painful.

Primary Need Seven: Elimination Of Waste

This is not a need which can be predicted by a child. Neither is it a need which is necessarily satisfied immediately — and finally — because a trip to the restroom has been allowed. And it is a need that cannot be denied. We also need to realize that some children are embarrassed or afraid to use school restrooms. If toilet doors have been removed, some students may feel comfortable using restrooms only during class time when they are empty. Too, if restrooms are hangouts for a bully or a gang, some students may be afraid to go in during passing periods.

Summary

The primary needs affect how students come to class and react while in class. If a student comes to school hungry, tired, or burdened with the countless problems that can exist at home, school and its demands are secondary. In fact, such feelings can foster resentments, cause hatred toward happy classmates, and generate anti-school attitudes. Then, having a teacher who seems oblivious to this personal void can produce student feelings that range from disinterest to hate. It's not difficult to see why.

Students who cause the most trouble in class may be struggling with a primary need. Sometimes, simply by demonstrating an awareness or small consideration, we can help the situation. That's why we must observe students in the halls, restrooms, and cafeterias as well as in class. After all, some kids don't have lunch money, others give their food away, and still others don't eat a bite. Much can be learned about children, and how to relate to them and teach them self-discipline, simply by watching them. Remember, restrooms need constant checking, just as academic progress does. Knowing that the primary needs must be met before good behavior and learning can ever seem meaningful to students is all the motivation we should need to keep close track of them. In truth, there isn't one of these needs that a teacher can't help with or alleviate. We may have to seek help or be the referral agent, but we have both the power and the resources to be advocates for children in this regard. In the process, we may turn many students who are discipline problems into working and academically productive students simply by meeting their primary needs.

PART THREE

THE SECONDARY NEEDS

Rationale: There are eight secondary needs, and it is within these needs that children can be motivated to study and learn as well as to behave in appropriate rather than inappropriate ways.

The primary needs discussed in the last chapter precede the possibility of motivating kids to behave properly. The secondary needs are the motivators themselves. There's no way a teacher can effectively get students to be disciplined without an awareness of — and effort toward appealing to — the secondary needs. When it comes to behavior and academic learning, they are the foundation of individual student discipline.

Where Teacher Influence In Changing Behavior Really Begins

Also called derived needs, they are psychological and, most important to a teacher, learned. Although the intensity of these needs varies from student to student, they are within us all. It's the secondary needs that motivate people to reach for goals, good or bad, and raise their self-concept — by our standards or theirs. Often, failure to aim our teaching toward these needs lies at the core of our ineffectiveness. Many times, the problem is that rather than fill these needs for students, we fight them. Worse, we may try to deny fulfillment of these needs and think such action is good. Yet, to be successful, one must search for the individual need — and then try to fill it in positive, constructive, and appropriate ways.

The secondary needs are:

Gregariousness	Aggression
Affiliation	Inquisitiveness
Achievement	Power
Status	Autonomy

Secondary Need One: Gregariousness

This is the need to associate with a group — to be in the "inner circle." It's revealed as a strong need by those students who are always organizing something, coming to your room after school, keeping you informed, and asking continually if they can help you. It's also a strong need in those who join a gang and fight school authorities. If you fulfill their need, you will motivate them effectively. If you don't, students will form their own structure or look elsewhere to meet this need. Look out your window some morning before school. You'll see kids who are not successful in school "hanging around" a specific area with a certain group of students.

Secondary Need Two: Aggression

This is the need to assert. For some students, it's the driving force in their lives. That's why you must give students assertive allowances in the classroom. Children are revealing a strong assertive need when they pester you about a new plan, want to do things that aren't in the book, or fight authority. If you can't let them meet this need in the classroom, they'll look to other activities in and out of class where they can be assertive. The "stand up, sit down, raise you hand" teacher who never offers variety drives these students crazy.

Secondary Need Three: Affiliation

Affiliation is the need we have to be "close" to the boss, peers, or the school. Students who join every club, participate frequently in class discussion, and volunteer continually have a strong affiliation need. If you're aloof or fail to acknowledge their interest, these students will dislike and avoid you. With touch and confirmation, they'll hang on every word you say. Take a close look at friendship and gang associations. Some kids would do "anything" to get into, or remain in, a gang. They have a need for affiliation.

Secondary Need Four: Inquisitiveness

The reason we always need to tell certain students what we're going to do is to meet their need of inquisitiveness. Good students almost always have a strong need in this regard. Others will never be interested in class work if this need can't be met by the activity. This need is also demonstrated by students who question everything, shoot holes in plans, or want you to look at everything they do. If you don't or won't tell these students the "whys," you'll turn them off. A close look will reveal that many problem students freely tell us all the "whys" of their misbehavior — as well as why a gang, rather than studying and being interested in school, is important.

Secondary Need Five: Achievement

This is the need to succeed — and to be recognized for achievement. Too often, athletic achievement is recognized in a school, but academic achievement is not — especially daily classroom achievements. In fact, we may tell students after a successful effort that they haven't proved anything yet. Those students who are always tooting their own horns, want grades posted, and seek constant approval have strong achievement needs. If you don't help students win and give them recognition for their successes, you will not motivate them effectively. A close look will reveal that many kids meet their achievement needs by telling us all the bad things they have done and are going to do. There are many children who fulfill this need by fighting. And their stakes for fighting also include peer recognition for fighting teachers.

Secondary Need Six: Power

Power is one of the stronger motivators. Behind every social movement — union, minority, women's, and all the rest — has been the need for power and the sharing of ownership. People want a measure of control over their lives. Students are not the exception. Therefore, if you try to dominate students, many will fight you. Some students, if they cannot be leaders in the school setting, will form their own structure where they can have power. Likewise, some kids get power by being bullies or by teasing, bossing, or controlling younger students.

Secondary Need Seven: Status

Everybody wants to be a somebody. This is the need for status. Students who reveal a strong status need include those who brag as well as those who are easily insulted, get mad when the class is punished because of a classmate, and want to know information before others do. To motivate these students, class activities must give them status — and any de-identification effort will make them angry. Remember, young people must have a name, not a number. You don't teach a class, you teach individuals in the class. The need for status is our individualism revealed, and it is a powerful force in some students.

Secondary Need Eight: Autonomy

Autonomy is the need to have our own way. It's the need to have input. This is not always possible in the classroom, of course. That's all the more reason our efforts must be inclusive — and considerate. Too, it's the reason we must share power in the classroom at every opportunity. Then, we can choose the power to bestow rather than deal with students trying to seize power. Remember, if it's the teacher's class, teacher's books, teacher's room, and teacher's lesson — then students think, "There is nothing in the classroom for me as a student." A close look will reveal that all studies indicate that *all students* do better in school if they determine their own goals to some extent and are involved in the decision-making process.

Summary

These eight psychological needs must never be ignored. They are the keys to both individual and group motivation. That's why we must study and learn every facet and interpretation of these needs as they relate to our efforts to discipline and to teach. Without giving these needs attention, we may find that orders, commands, and demands are necessary to achieve our every desire in the classroom. If we treat these needs as unnecessary considerations, we may find dissent and insubordination at our door. Remember, neither has to be "out in the open" to be in existence.

Failure to aim our teaching toward individual human needs leads to big misconceptions. We tend to believe that teaching is telling. It is not. Too, we're likely to believe all students are the same. They are not. All of our students are products of their environments and experiences — past, present, and anticipated. Likewise, the intensity of each need differs within us all. Therefore, differences lie at the base of the secondary motives for each student. That's why needs are the first cause to consider when our teaching is being ignored or rejected. Remember, rejection of our teaching or school — whether revealed in an academic or behavior problem — is usually absolutely and totally personal.

Unless we devote time to discovering and meeting each student's unique needs, our efforts to discipline students may parallel going fishing without any bait. We can begin by looking at our students individually. Then, we may try to determine which needs individual students most want fulfilled. By using these needs as positive motivators, we may begin our most successful efforts in handling misbehavior. Therefore, our task is to find the need — and fill it.

PART FOUR

THE PRIMARY CAUSES OF MISBEHAVIOR

Rationale: All behavior — appropriate and inappropriate — has purpose. Attention, power, revenge, and self-confidence are the primary causes of both appropriate and inappropriate behavior.

The primary and secondary needs are vital considerations in changing unacceptable behavior to acceptable behavior. They offer a teacher clues to the causes of misbehavior, and also suggest action to change that behavior. Yet, four needs cause the majority of problems: attention, power, revenge, and self-confidence. In addition to the primary and secondary needs, they are offered here for a very important reason.

Perhaps more than any other obstacle in teaching, discipline problems cause us to be less effective than we could be. They can make us give up and quit on some kids. Discipline problems can cause us to make rules for the majority to control the minority. They can cause us to be mean, sarcastic, and hateful toward some students — and maybe toward a whole class. That's why discipline problems are so important. In truth, if they didn't affect teachers in such destructive ways, they wouldn't hold so much significance. But they do. Even one discipline problem can affect us in a negative way. That's why our need to learn and understand more about discipline and behavior is so vitally important.

All Behavior, Appropriate And Inappropriate, Has Purpose

A teacher must never forget that all behavior has purpose. The student who behaves in acceptable ways does so for a reason. Likewise, the student who behaves in unacceptable ways does so for a reason. If we would spend as much time with the reasons for misbehavior as we do with punishments for misbehavior, more discipline problems would be resolved.

The fact that all misbehavior has purpose is the primary reason we can't lump all discipline problems under one label and treat them the same way. It won't work. The bully does not have the same motivations for misbehavior as the class clown. The late arriver is different from the student who talks back to a teacher. The defiant student may have a different motivation than the student who talks all the time.

In maintaining a successful approach to changing unacceptable behavior to acceptable behavior, teachers must never forget that the first step to solution lies in discovering the purpose of the misbehavior. It's a fact: Teachers cannot treat *any misbehavior* until they know the reasons for it. That is, they can't if they want to change the behavior.

To say that there are only four sources of misbehavior would be untrue. However, these are four primary causes of misbehavior: attention, power, revenge, and self-confidence. If we could learn to handle misbehavior resulting from these four needs, the majority of our classroom discipline problems would be resolved. If we could remember the primary and secondary needs, many discipline problems wouldn't even come to be.

Attention

Most students gain attention through normal channels. However, for some students, misbehavior is the *only* source of attention. Most commonly, these are the students who speak out without permission, arrive late for class, or make strange noises which force class and teacher attention. Some students will even tell us all the bad things they have done. They are all misbehaving for the purpose of gaining attention. Attention is the need which must be met. If they cannot get attention in appropriate ways, they will misbehave. Remember, attention reduces potential problems and cures current ones. Look at your class roster and try to determine which children are prone to misbehave to gain attention.

Power

The need for power also is a primary cause of misbehavior. Students express this need by open dissent, by refusal to follow rules, or by being controversial. Remember, these students usually feel defeated if they do as they are told. Most commonly, we know these students as the total independents, the defiant ones, the rule breakers, and the bullies. They truly feel more power is the answer to all their problems. They believe that if they had more power, nobody could tell them to do anything; they would be doing the telling. The purpose of their misbehavior is to gain power; therefore, the need for power is what must be treated. If they cannot gain power in appropriate ways, they will fight for it in inappropriate ways. Look at your class roster and determine which students are revealing a power need through their behavior.

Revenge

Some students find their places by being disliked, feared, or hated. As teachers, what we need to know about these students in order to change their behavior is that failure has made them give up trying for attention or power via socially accepted methods. Unfortunately, they find personal satisfaction in being mean, vicious, and violent. The purpose of their misbehavior is revenge. They are the students who write on desks, beat up classmates, threaten young students, cause constant controversy, and mar restroom walls. They will seek revenge against teachers and classmates in any way they can. Therefore, revenge is the behavior which must be treated. If you have students who fall into misbehaving because they are seeking revenge, realize that only appropriate success will change them.

Self-Confidence

A lack of self-confidence is also a cause for misbehavior — and a very common one. Students who lack self-confidence honestly expect failure. They frustrate teachers because they are often capable of handling their studies successfully. We are angered because we feel their behavior is a cop-out. In some ways it is. Regardless, these students use inability or assumed inability to escape participation. When they are supposed to be studying, they play and talk to others. Then, they offer "I couldn't do it," or "I don't know how" as an excuse. Remember, lack of self-confidence is the cause of the misbehavior *regardless* of how it is being manifested. It is the real issue and, therefore, must be treated. Again, only success can change these students' self-image.

Summary

To resolve discipline problems, a teacher must remember that all student behavior — good and bad — has purpose. Until we recognize the purposes of misbehavior, we can never be positioned to deal with it effectively. And this is significant because a close look will reveal that discipline problems aren't the real source of our anxiety. It's our inability to cope with them that causes our frustration and despair.

There are four needs that are primary causes of misbehavior: attention, power, revenge, and self-confidence. That's why we must identify the purposes of misbehavior individually. Once these purposes are identified, students needing *attention* must receive it in positive ways to prevent their seeking it in disruptive ways. We should recognize that giving *power* to those students who need it is easy — and with it comes the perfect opportunity to teach that responsibility is a part of power. Understand that the *revenge seekers* can be diverted back to the healthy goals they have abandoned out of despair, if they are given a sense of place and belonging. They cannot be ignored or rejected, or their hate will remain. Finally, those who misbehave because of feelings of *inferiority* can be changed by success. However, minor or insignificant tasks will increase their anxieties — while succeeding at important tasks will increase their self-esteem.

Unless we respond professionally to misbehavior, we are not positioned to manage discipline problems. When we take the misbehavior of students personally, we are likely to respond in ways that we will regret. It's at this point — reacting personally — that we stop solving our discipline problems and start being consumed by them.

CHAPTER

2

STRATEGIC ATTITUDE

PART ONE

THE IMPORTANCE OF STRATEGIC ATTITUDE

A professional strategic attitude is of vital importance to a teacher's success. It affects teacher efficiency with all students, including those who are discipline problems. It also offers continuous perspective in negative situations and, therefore, helps determine our happiness, satisfaction, and well-being. Our strategic attitude must include adopting a professional management stance.

Many teachers do not regard themselves as management. Rather, they think only of administrators as management. Yet, it's this precise thinking that may be the reason some teachers do not develop the correct strategic attitude and do not experience the level of success they should with discipline problems. That's because the classroom teacher *is* management. Whenever you manage work, you are management. Whenever you manage the people who must do that work, you are management. Whenever you teach desirable attitudes, skills, and appropriate behavior to people, you are management. As classroom teachers, we do all three for students.

The Teacher As Management

To gain maximum satisfaction and productivity in the classroom, a teacher simply must think and function as management. Therefore, both our strategic attitudes and our skills in the management arena need continuous developing and perfecting. In truth, all the laws of management which govern school administrators and business executives also govern the classroom teacher. When it comes to managing the work, behavior, and achievements of students, these laws apply.

We may respond, "This is too much responsibility for any teacher to shoulder." Yet, a close look will reveal that the laws of management are the reality for the teacher in the classroom, whether we like it or not. For example, anyone in a management position must accept total responsibility for everything that happens under his or her leadership — and for good reason. If students can't read, do they get the blame? No, we do. If students are misbehaving or not taking the right courses to enter college or get a job, do people blame students? No, they blame us. This is the reason our strategic attitudes are so vital — to us as well as to students.

We, as classroom teachers, are management in every sense of the word. Therefore, all the management laws relative to leading people and accomplishing work are prerequisites for successful teaching. The teacher is more than a token manager. He or she is the chief executive officer in the classroom.

Summary

Management laws must be a part of our strategic attitudes. These laws are aids; they serve as constant guides for operating in the classroom. In the most difficult situations, they serve as guideposts for the teacher thinking and action which give the highest probability of success.

When we violate these laws, problems are inevitable. And often, the reason for our violation is that we are not even aware of them — much less ready to think in management terms. Once we adopt strategic management attitudes, however, we are positioned to manage. Equally important, thinking of ourselves as management gives us the control and flexibility we need to take positive and constructive action in every classroom and school situation — including discipline situations — every day of the year.

PART TWO

THE LAWS AND PRINCIPLES: AN EXPLANATION

Professional attitudes are paramount to teacher success. In fact, there is a direct correlation between a teacher's attitude and his or her stability and effectiveness in discipline situations. Most of the guidelines for adopting highly successful professional attitudes lie in a teacher's knowing, understanding, and following seven laws of management. These seven laws are the foundation of a teacher's professional strategic attitude for gaining acceptable student behavior as well as handling misbehavior when it occurs.

However, I think you need to know the source of these laws before giving them weight. I wrote these laws and put a name on them. Yet, in reality, they are not my creations. Rather, they are natural laws. Therefore, I didn't create them. Rather, I just brought them into an identifiable form with a practical application for teachers.

In a way, these laws are like economic laws. Nobody created them. They just describe the way things work. So it is with these laws and principles I have written. In successful classrooms, teachers are applying these laws naturally — whether they know them or not. In classrooms where teachers are failing, they are probably doing *exactly* the opposite of what these laws teach. In fact, these teachers are probably making every mistake in the book, and not even realizing it. Worse, they may be blaming everyone else for what's wrong insofar as discipline problems are concerned. That's why these laws need your consideration.

The laws and principles are guideposts to use in every discipline situation. They will give you automatic vision and direction. They will help in every decision-making situation. In addition, the laws have personal value to you. They assure consistency of effort. They agree with sound educational practices and offer constant direction which is student-centered. Equally important, they provide a *conditioned response* — an immediately available and automatic course of action — in problem situations. This means the laws give you a personal and professional support system in *every* discipline situation.

The laws and principles also take the trial and error out of teacher action because they are objective, not subjective, and offer action which gives a teacher the highest probability of success. Finally, they reveal our human normalcy in experiencing problems as well as the normalcy of student behavior, therefore reducing our fear or need to react defensively. The laws and principles are the beginning foundation for professional strategic attitudes which facilitate success in all leadership situations, including discipline problems.

PART THREE

THE LAW OF ORIGIN

Strategic Attitude Rationale: Institutions — and the people who work in them — must operate in agreement with the reason for their origin and existence, or failure, rather than success, becomes the probability — for the individual and the institution.

This is not an institutional theory. It is a law. It applies to businesses, families, churches, and schools. It applies to carpenters, bricklayers, corporate executives, school administrators, and teachers. Without doubt, it is a management absolute in education. Failure to adhere to this law will get teachers in trouble with more people, more quickly, than any other thing they can do. It can result in the destruction of the individual as well as the school's credibility.

In truth, teacher action which violates this law reflects an incompetency and obvious misdirection that is, indeed, reason for termination. Little can or will be achieved in the presence of this inconsistency of direction and purpose — quite the contrary. Constant personal and professional conflicts, a division of staff, and student and public unrest will be the ever-present school condition. When this law is not followed, discipline problems in the classroom are inevitable. Worse, the resolution of discipline problems is almost impossible without both constant supervision of students and continually applied force. That's the reality produced by a violation of the Law of Origin.

Teacher decision making and discipline action that contradict the Law of Origin are always without defense. On the other hand, compliance with this law not only assures proper direction, but also provides educators with the foundation and skills to make and defend decisions that are consistent with good educational and student-centered practices. This law must be entrenched like a rock in our strategic professional attitudes, and practiced faithfully. It is the foundation of our appointment to the professional position we hold as educators. This law has far-reaching dimensions which begin before discipline problems arise. Indeed, this law is our best preventive medicine for curtailing misbehavior. That's why we need to look at the comprehensiveness of this law rather than just look at its specific applications to discipline problems.

A Student-Centered School

A school must be student-centered. This is a simple, yet all-encompassing, fact inherent in the reason for the existence of schools and, therefore, inherent in the work of the school. Everything we do in a school — whether it's planning lessons or handling a discipline problem — must be in the best interest of children. We simply must be ever aware that schools were not created to employ teachers, psychologists, cooks, secretaries, custodians, counselors, administrators — or anyone else. Schools were created to meet the needs of students.

Recent years have brought forth a new feeling among some educators. The school, they say, can't do everything. Teachers are overworked and underpaid. All this may be true, but the school must be very careful in placing limits on what it will or will not do to meet the needs of students. That's because when the school places limits on what it will do, it places limits on its very being and effectiveness as well. The same is true for the individual teacher.

The school is a large part of every community. It is a focal point in the lives of parents as well as children. Young people don't have much of a chance for success in this world of ours without schools and an education. That's why the school must be careful in making proclamations about what it will not do for those it was created to serve. Such action by any institution is the first step in bringing people to decide there is no need to support that institution by word or deed. And schools need both forms of public support to be successful.

As workers of the school, our competency as well as our security is totally and directly linked to how effectively the school can meet the needs of students. This is neither rhetoric nor theory. It is truth. Any time we become teacher-centered or administrator-centered, or centered in any direction other than that of students' best interest, we have lost sight of the reason for our existence. That's a violation of the Law of Origin — and it's dangerous. That's when we can begin to make big mistakes, including mistakes with discipline problems, in both our thinking and our action. Remember, the school was meant to meet the needs of all children — bright, slow, interested, disinterested, well-behaved, and ill-behaved.

The Law of Origin operates on every level for every worker of the school — from custodians to teachers to the board of education. Unfortunately, there are many ways we can violate the Law of Origin. For instance, if we decide to clean classrooms at the time convenient for custodians rather than at the time of students' best interest, we are custodian-centered in this case. These kinds of decisions are not uncommon. Often, access to gyms, auditoriums, and classrooms is denied students because of the cleaning schedules of custodians. Make no mistake, this is a violation of the Law of Origin. True, it may be inconvenient and difficult to arrange schedules and get custodians to work at certain times in order to work around the needs of students. Yet, a school is either student-centered or it is not. And when it comes to managing discipline problems, a strategic professional attitude which is student-centered rather than teacher-centered will give the highest probability of success.

Other examples of violations of this law can be seen when a film is not shown in a classroom because a projector would be difficult to locate or would have to be transported from another place, or activities are eliminated because a faculty sponsor cannot be found. Flexible scheduling may be disallowed because teachers don't want it, or an assembly may not be scheduled for fear teachers would be angered by the interruption. In all these instances, students' best interest has been overlooked or ignored for one reason or another. In each case, students' best interest has been placed in a position secondary to the wants and needs of someone else. That's a dangerous situation for either a school or educators to be in. These kinds of deviations can develop into big contradictions when one does not understand the full meaning of the Law of Origin.

When a teacher violates this law by leaning in one direction or another — for any reason — the position of that teacher and the institution is jeopardized. Everything from teacher ability, to judgment, to credibility, is subject to question and criticism. In truth, it should be. However, no matter what we do, if we truly believe our actions to be in the best interest of students, our actions are at least defensible. Even when we err, if we can show that we believed our actions were in the best interest of students, we are in a defensible position. In most cases, you will find that our problems come when we do what may have been best for someone else — but wasn't in the best interest of students.

Reflected In Every Decision

Every teacher action must be in agreement with the reason for the existence and origin of the institution. In discipline situations, adopting this strategic attitude is a must. When it is not adopted, the stage is set for failure.

Adopting this strategic attitude also includes the establishment of necessary rules and regulations as day-to-day operation guides for teachers in fulfilling the mission of our creation and existence.

It's not uncommon for educators to talk in one direction and act in another, especially when the subject applies to them. Of course, this is easily detected by students and everyone else. Administrators may tell teachers to be student-centered when they ask them to do something — regardless of the extra work — then refuse to allow a unit of study or offer an extra course, or eliminate a student-centered service because it takes too much administrative time and would involve too much red tape. Likewise, teachers may tell students to work hard — and say, "If you don't work hard, you will not be successful." Then, these same students may see teachers negotiating for more money and shorter work days.

These types of contradictions by educators can and will begin causing student doubts, and spread to a general feeling of discontent. Such violations of the Law of Origin may culminate in problems that grow beyond solution. Remember, all efforts must support and promote the fulfillment of the Law of Origin goal. Any deviation is a mistake — a mistake serious enough to bring failure.

One may say, "We will always have schools." This is probably true. Yet, there is a difference between schools that are allowed to exist and ones that are encouraged by public support to flourish and grow. Remember, people may tolerate an institution when it has lost sight of its purpose, but they will not support it to the degree required for it to prosper and thrive. Maybe this is one of the reasons schools always seem to be in a financial crisis. Never forget, the public doesn't care that the institution satisfies the wants and needs of the workers of that institution — unless the workers are fulfilling the needs of the people. That's a fact.

Summary

Practicing the Law of Origin facilitates making teaching a function rather than a position. We see our role as educators in perspective, and the direction of our efforts is clear — not only to us but also to those we lead. The Law of Origin facilitates the acceptance of teacher decisions, planning, and leadership more than any other management law. On the other hand, if we are teacher-centered or administrator-centered or athletics-centered, nothing the institution does seems to make any sense.

Every decision must be preceded by the question, "Is it good for students?" When all our decisions answer this question in agreement with the Law of Origin, everything from new lessons to rules and regulations has purpose, direction, reason, and a common-sense foundation.

Too, it is the Law of Origin that gives teachers, individually and collectively, a common objective. It gives all a base for decision making in any problem situation — be it a discipline problem or a question of failing a student. It also gives us a system of checks and balances. Teacher orders, directives, and decisions are seen as facilitating the work of the students, rather than facilitating the work of teachers without regard to the effect on the students' work. Students are willing to follow because teacher efforts make sense when they are in agreement with the reason for the existence of the institution. In truth, it is when we attempt to lead in contradiction to the Law of Origin that the majority of our problems begin. That's why the acceptance of this law is the first requirement of those who intend to teach and manage a classroom of students. It must be accepted by teachers, or they will fail to recognize the reason for their existence. Accepting and practicing this law is paramount in discipline situations. Therefore, the Law of Origin is vital to your professional strategic attitude. The welfare of students *must* be your fundamental value in every discipline situation.

PART FOUR

THE LAW OF TOTAL RESPONSIBILITY

Strategic Attitude Rationale: The Law of Total Responsibility states that the teacher is responsible for everything that happens within his or her classroom. This principle applies to every level of appointed leadership in a school or district.

It's a fact: A principal or superintendent is responsible for everything that happens in a school or system. The administrator, whether responsible for an individual school or the entire district, is the one looked to by the public, students, and teachers as accountable and responsible for all. If you doubt this truth, recall what happens when something goes wrong. Whether a boiler blows up or a teacher mistreats a student — or a student throws an egg on a passing automobile — a principal or superintendent will be the one who gets the call. Worse, if the situation cannot be corrected or mended, the administrator will receive the blame.

The same is true in the classroom. If students fail, do people blame students? No, they blame the teacher. If a class is unruly, it's the teacher — not the students — who is faulted. These examples are offered to prove the point of a vitally important management principle. This management philosophy is called the Law of Total Responsibility.

Totally Responsible...For Everything

This management principle is all-inclusive. It relates that an appointed leader is responsible for everything that happens within that realm of leadership. Therefore, a teacher is responsible for everything that happens in his or her classroom. Right or wrong, good or bad, fair or unfair — that's the way it is and that's the way it will always be. In truth, it can be no other way. The important thing is for every teacher to accept the reality of this responsibility from a positive and constructive point of view. This is the challenge and excitement inherent in teaching. It is also the burden of appointed leadership.

Classroom teaching is not a place for the weak or those who cannot accept the authority that goes with total responsibility. The problem results for the individual teacher as well as the institution when the appointed leader cannot or will not accept this management principle. It is the failure to accept this principle that causes a breakdown in both responsibility and performance within an organization. A stagnation of the people as well as the institution is the least serious result that a failure to accept this management principle can produce. Regression is the most common effect. The ultimate result, of course, is the destruction of the institution itself. This is not an uncommon occurrence. Experience will reveal the destruction of entire organizations has resulted because leadership failed to accept total responsibility for everything from finances to policy. And we've all seen teachers fail in the classroom because they could not accept total responsibility for what was occurring in it, including learning and discipline problems.

However, once the Law of Total Responsibility is accepted as a part of your strategic attitude, it changes your entire viewpoint, perspective, and approach. Remember, the point is that an appointed leader is responsible for everything.

A Requirement For Problem Solving

When a classroom is headed by a teacher who does not practice this principle, there is no sense of direction for the teacher or those being led. Most importantly, adhering to this management principle encourages and facilitates an attempt at problem solving, rather than merely a recognition that a problem exists. Needless to say, it also results in problems being solved.

When teachers do not accept and adhere to this principle, problems in the classroom may be identified, but they are usually allowed to exist undisturbed. This is true because nobody feels, or is willing to accept, responsibility for the problem or situation. Rather, we tend to adopt the practice of blaming others for a problem, and absolve ourselves of all guilt and responsibility for any situation. Then, we voluntarily remove ourselves mentally from the leadership position to which we were appointed. Thus, we can't deal with the problem or the work for which we have leadership responsibility. We say, "Don't look at me; that's the math department's (or the coach's) fault," or "Johnny just can't behave." The problem is that the difficulty remains.

In management, when the person of lesser authority does not perform, responsibility for that failure always reverts upward — not downward. It never remains static. Never forget this reality in any discipline situation.

If a student is not performing in the classroom, the teacher must move in. The teacher who fails to assume a personal and professional attitude of responsibility for everything that happens within the classroom will never be a totally accepted leader. Such teachers may be able to develop the skills which enable them to identify discipline problems accurately, but they will never be problem solvers. Final responsibility always rests at the highest point in any organization, and unless this management philosophy is accepted, the Law of Total Responsibility cannot be effected. In the classroom, the teacher is the learning leader.

On Every Level

Remember, the Law of Total Responsibility operates on every level. For example, students are responsible for their actions, yet the teacher is responsible for all things they do, or do not do, well. Likewise, teachers are responsible for their own ability, actions, and/or behavior. However, the department head is responsible too. The Law of Total Responsibility always reverts to the top where, of course, the principal is responsible for all — students, teachers, department heads, and the rest of the school team. The superintendent is responsible for everything that happens within the entire school system.

The Law of Total Responsibility does not imply that responsibility and authority cannot or should not be delegated. Quite the contrary: It simply means that when anyone in a position of delegated responsibility fails to perform, the responsibility for taking action to correct that failure automatically reverts upward at that point. That's why teaching is a function, not a position. If a teacher sees the job as merely the filling of a slot, then many of his or her responsibilities will revert to the principal. When we fail to follow this management principle, failure tends to become permanent because nobody ever corrects the situation. A department head doesn't call any meeting — so there is never a meeting. A teacher is failing too many students — and continues to fail more students.

Summary

The total responsibility concept is an extremely simple, yet all-encompassing, principle of management. When it is absent from leadership action, a close look will reveal that the person at the lowest responsibility level is usually blamed first for any failure. Worse, both the blame and the problem are allowed to remain because nobody at the higher level is willing to assume responsibility for the existing conditions. When this is the case, there is no leadership at all. This is the real problem. It is not uncommon, especially in discipline situations.

However, when teachers accept and practice the Law of Total Responsibility, control and a sense of responsibility are always maintained within an institution. Most important, control and responsibility can never be lost because responsibility always continues to revert in an upward direction. Loose ends are eliminated. True, students must be helped and encouraged to solve their own problems, for they too must understand and accept the total responsibility concept. Yet, if a student becomes stymied or falters for any reason, the responsibility for help or correction lies with the teacher, then the department head, and then the principal. The problem is never left to exist or to be perpetuated.

Whether the student's problem be with academics or behavior, the teacher must assume the management position of total responsibility. That is, we must if success is to be achieved. When this principle is not accepted, unfinished business and a void in the solution of problems become the rule of the day. When this happens, guess who receives the blame. You're right — the teacher. And that's exactly where the blame should lie — with the one responsible for everything that happens within the classroom. And if the teacher fails, who gets blamed? That's right, the principal — for not doing anything. And if a principal doesn't perform, guess who gets blamed — the superintendent. That's why this is a principle of management that applies to all leaders.

Accepting and practicing this law is paramount in discipline situations. Therefore, the Law of Total Responsibility is vital to your professional strategic attitude.

PART FIVE

THE LAW OF EVER-PRESENT LEADERSHIP

Strategic Attitude Rationale: Whenever two or more people gather, leadership is present. This resulting leadership may be a positive or negative force in the lives of individuals as well as the work of the institution.

Many teachers ignore or overlook this overwhelmingly important leadership law. Others feel that their position and title alone denote to students that they are the source of leadership within a classroom.

In many ways, this kind of thinking can result in some vital management misconceptions, especially if the teacher assumes there is no need for one to establish and maintain his or her position with students. Such teachers are likely to believe that, when all else fails, an order, demand, or directive will cause students to follow their leadership or correct any situation. If these teachers would look more closely, they might see that titles which denote positions of leadership, such as teacher, department head, team leader, principal, or superintendent, can sometimes be secondary and even insignificant in the *actual leadership* in a classroom or school.

Two Kinds Of Leadership

Basically, there are only two kinds of leadership: appointed and emerging. The appointed leader is the individual who has the legal title, authority, and responsibility to effectively carry out the work of the school. The classroom teacher is a prime example for our discussion here. However, when appointed leaders do not take charge of the responsibilities inherent in their granted positions, leadership will *always* emerge from the group that the appointed leader should be directing. This is the Law of Ever-Present Leadership. The basic truth of this law is one that every teacher must remember when dealing with students.

The Law of Ever-Present Leadership can result in a loss of appointed leadership which may be temporary or permanent. In truth, whether the loss is permanent or not is determined to a great extent by the emerging leader. If the emerging leader has the desire to accept permanent leadership rather than follow the appointed leader, it is his or hers for the taking. Fortunately, a student may take leadership on one issue and then refuse the leadership on another issue that classmates attempt to impose on him or her. On the other hand, a student may become leader in the classroom, not in title, but in reality. We've all seen administrators lose their leadership to a member or members of the teaching staff. And we've all seen teachers lose their positions in the classroom to one student. That's the Law of Ever-Present Leadership revealed.

Negative Leadership Is The Probability

Emerging leadership may be either positive or negative. Sometimes emerging leadership is good. Unfortunately, most often it is not. The reason negative rather than positive leadership most often emerges from a group is twofold.

First, people of equal rank, such as the rest of the faculty or the rest of the class, are very unlikely to "speak out" against each other to defend a "non-acting" or absent appointed leader. This is not abnormal behavior. It is simply the common way people react in the presence of peers. A teacher must never discount the force of peer pressures within a class. If one student is telling classmates about "all the mistakes and wrongs" that exist in a particular situation, or "what kids shouldn't have to do," or "how imcompetent the teacher is," it is very likely that even those students who usually support the teacher, for instance, would say nothing. They may not join the negative discussion and participate, but neither are they likely to disagree or correct the thinking of a classmate to defend the teacher. True, they may. However, their stance is more likely to be silence. They may be angered. But to speak out in support of the teacher and against a classmate in the presence of peer pressure is the exception rather than the rule. If you think not, you haven't heard all the talk among students. The same is true of teachers. It is not common for them to defend an administrator in similar circumstances. A teacher should not be angered or disappointed when such events take place. This is simply people reacting in a human way.

Second, negative leadership emerges most often because the students who gain authority within a group — without a corresponding degree of accountable responsibility to some higher authority — are most likely to act and react out of self-interest rather than in the best interest of the class or of those the institution serves. Students are not different from us in this respect. This is exactly what happens in many teacher lounge discussions. They end in criticisms approaching insubordination.

Examples of emerging leadership in schools are countless. An emerging leader simply "takes" or is "given" leadership. After gaining the authority and power granted by the group, the emerging leader usually proceeds in the misguided direction of self-interest rather than student and class interest.

In many instances, it is through emerging colleague leadership that teachers begin to accept teacher-centered rather than student-centered attitudes and practices. A negative leader simply has emerged from the group and begins feeding colleagues negative, self-directed, unprofessional thoughts. In the classroom, one student can do the same thing.

They May Mean Well

Don't be misled; this negative emerging leader may be well-meaning. A student, for instance, truly may not be fully aware of the discord he or she brings. Too, he or she may be ''pushed'' or ''forced'' into a leadership role by classmates. The same is true of teachers. I have always wondered, ''If this outspoken and misdirected emerging leader were suddenly made principal, would he or she say those same things in the same way to colleagues at the faculty meeting tomorrow?'' I think not. Why? Because once one is made an appointed leader, *accountable responsibility* has been added to authority. This fact changes the entire situation.

Without doubt, the best counteraction to decrease power and effectiveness of negative emerging student leadership is for appointed leaders to meet their leadership responsibilities. Please note that I said, ''negative emerging leadership,'' for we are constantly striving to encourage the emergence of positive student leaders. We could not operate without them. Yet, we give these student leaders authority *and* responsibility. They remain accountable to us — the appointed leaders. However, the chance of positive emerging leadership developing without positive appointed leadership is slim.

A Powerful Force

A teacher must never ignore or discount emerging student leadership. Its force in the classroom can be overwhelming. A teacher who can accept the Law of Ever-Present Leadership immediately realizes that he or she, as the appointed leader, must make decisions and take action in all situations, discipline included. You can't sit on your hands and be an accepted or competent appointed leader. Too, a teacher must know that to be an effective disciplinarian, continuous communication with every student is an absolute necessity. In truth, one must realize that being granted a position as an appointed leader is no more than being given an open-ended opportunity to prove that the right appointment was made or was not made. No guarantees come with the appointment.

Respect cannot be granted by appointment or title. One must work continually at earning leadership acknowledgment and respect from students. Certainly, respect is not something that a teacher can demand, force, or insist upon. It must be earned.

Summary

None of us who are now teachers were always appointed leaders. Our experience should tell us that leadership acceptance and respect can be achieved best by example as well as by providing tangible evidence of help, direction, and assistance to those we lead. Unless we are willing to be an example of good leadership to students by word as well as deed, respect cannot be earned. Remember, I said *word* and *deed.* A teacher cannot find leadership success unless he or she actively provides students with the tools and skills they need to find success in the classroom. These tools and skills include more than books, desks, paper, and lesson plans. And students cannot be expected to look only to themselves to find success in the classroom.

Never forget, we all ask the same question of our leaders: "What are they doing for me?" If the answer is "Nothing," then those being led will look somewhere else for assistance as well as leadership. This is true for administrators and teachers as well as students. A principal looks to the superintendent and says, "What is he or she doing for me personally — to help me be a better principal and find happiness in the process?" Teachers ask the same question about principals and superintendents. Students ask the same question about their teachers. It's as personal as that. If the answer is "Nothing," then people look elsewhere for leadership. That's the effect of the Law of Ever-Present Leadership revealed. That's why, as teachers, we can never forget this law. If we do, we can lose both our function and our position, and everyone will know it.

Accepting and practicing this law is paramount in discipline situations. Therefore, the Law of Ever-Present Leadership is vital to your professional strategic attitude.

PART SIX

THE LAW OF POSITIVE REINFORCEMENT

Strategic Attitude Rationale: In the absence of positive reinforcement from appointed leaders, negative human attitudes and behaviors are most likely to emerge from the group being led.

This is not just a management law. It's also a law of human behavior. Unfortunately, the truth of this law is revealed often in both our personal and our professional lives. In a school, negative staff members are overwhelmingly frustrating and depressing for positive staff members. Negative students have the same effect upon their classmates and teachers. Yet, if negative student attitudes cannot be changed — or at least neutralized — the negative student may emerge as the strongest force within the classroom and school. That's the Law of Positive Reinforcement. It is this law which teaches us that an individual discipline problem can become a class discipline problem. And without positive teacher action, this process can be hard to stop. The same condition can exist within the faculty for similar reasons.

The Negative Dominates

Sometimes I am amazed that competent, intelligent, and positive teachers will sit in the teachers' lounge or a faculty meeting and listen while others offer every possible "I can't," "What's wrong," or "How terrible teaching is" — without offering even token resistance. Occasionally, good teachers will even pretend agreement rather than risk disagreement. Maybe this is another example of the power of peer pressure revealed.

Negative students have similar influence upon a class. Therefore, never forget that negative teacher attitudes can be overwhelmingly stifling and destructive to meeting the needs of students, accomplishing the work of the school, and effecting positive leadership in the process. A teacher simply must counter student negativism with concrete help and positive reinforcement. Allowing the continuation and perpetuation of negative student attitudes has an influence on the entire class.

A Vital Need

Yet, a teacher needs to understand negativism as well as those students who have a tendency to be negative. The primary and secondary needs discussed earlier provide valuable insights. Being negative is neither easy nor satisfying, however. It is difficult and unrewarding for anyone, including students, always to operate from the negative. It is so much easier to function from the positive. It's difficult to operate negatively because being negative is self-defeating and self-degrading. It is a horrible experience. All negative people realize this truth. They are not happy people. Worse, they don't know what to do about it. This lesson about positive and negative is one we need to teach all students for obvious reasons.

As teachers, we need to realize that being positive is vitally important to us as well as students. We need to realize that being negative is against everything education stands for. For every negative we offer, we give students *nothing*. On the other hand, for every positive we propose to kids, we have at least suggested a *possible course of action*. This is the basis for the practicality of, as well as the professional need for, the positive in the lives of educators and students alike.

The motivation, stimulation, and confidence needed to begin with a probability for success are impaired by the negative. People need positives — if for no other reason than to avoid being consumed by the certain depression and failure inherent in the negative. A teacher must understand and be concerned about positives. They are a tremendous force in the lives of educators and students.

The need for positives is a practical part of our everyday existence. Positives play a vital role in the development of the mental health, achievement, and behavior of those we lead. Without positives, hopelessness replaces hope. None of us can live with any happiness, satisfaction, or peace of mind if hope is denied. Rather, we live oppressed by what we have not done or what we have failed to try.

Summary

A teacher must recognize the fact that when we offer students a negative, in truth, we offer something worse than absolutely nothing. We impose an added burden which our students must overcome. That's why in our lives as teachers, we have a practical need for positives, and the Law of Positive Reinforcement should receive our constant attention. Applying this law must be a part of our professional strategic attitude.

We need to remember that our teaching is positive if we praise rather than condemn, suggest rather than demand, help rather than impose, share rather than tell, request rather than command, and counsel rather than force. We must never forget, even for a moment, that we should always be the positive element in the classroom scene. We must know that unless we reinforce the positive, negative student attitudes will flourish and may consume all the classroom — teacher and students alike.

Establishing a positive climate in the classroom is a teacher responsibility. We are the climate leaders in the classroom and school. The Law of Positive Reinforcement is a constant reminder that the negative will result unless we provide the impetus for the growth of the positive. If we don't function from the positive, "nothing" will be the tone of the classroom and "nothing" will be our primary accomplishment. Accepting and practicing this law is paramount in discipline situations. Therefore, the Law of Positive Reinforcement is paramount to your professional strategic attitude.

PART SEVEN

THE PRINCIPLE OF MANAGEMENT ADJUSTMENT

Strategic Attitude Rationale: To effect leadership in the classroom, a teacher must adjust his or her own behavior when attempting to get students to change their behavior. Without such adjustment, problems will not be corrected.

Many times appointed leaders, including teachers, believe that the higher one goes in rank, title, salary, and appointed position within an institution, the more subordinates must adjust to them. With this belief, of course, goes the attitude that the leader can and should be the boss. One is likely to believe that's the way it is supposed to be. Therefore, one is likely to believe that any adjusting done should be done by others — not the boss. This belief is totally false. Yet, many educators continue to believe that students should adjust to teachers, teachers to principals, principals to superintendents, etc. A close look will reveal that the opposite is true. That is, it is if one expects to lead other human beings.

The Principle of Management Adjustment teaches us that the higher one goes in title and position, the more he or she is required to adjust his or her behavior to get others to adjust theirs. In fact, the leader must be the primary adjustor. That's the lesson taught by the Principle of Management

Adjustment. In discipline situations, accepting this principle is an absolute for resolving problems.

The Primary Adjustor

The successful teacher finds quickly that it is he or she who must make adjustments to compensate for the strengths, weaknesses, beliefs, attitudes, opinions, behaviors, and skills of students. It is only through using learned knowledge about human behavior and evaluating the skills of students — and then making adjustments — that leadership can be effected. That's a fact. The teacher must *always* be the primary adjustor in discipline situations. When this is not the leadership practice, discipline problems may be approached and even reprimanded, but they don't get solved.

The teacher attitude that "I'm the boss and that's the way it's going to be" only promotes fight or flight on the part of students. It seldom stimulates or motivates students to change behavior. It is a teacher's responsibility to utilize the methods and techniques which make students move in the desired direction. This can be achieved only by adjustment. This is both the challenge and the responsibility of teaching and managing a classroom. If a teacher holds rigid and can't make adjustments in method, technique, and behavior to motivate students — with some measure of success — he or she will never find success in teaching. Remember, the only way you can ever get students to adjust their behavior is to first adjust your own.

Summary

When a teacher cannot or will not make adjustments, any problem solving is temporary — at best. The teacher who says, "We do it this way just because I'm the boss," finds out quickly that this approach doesn't work. It never will. That's the Principle of Management Adjustment revealed. To get students to do what we want them to do requires one prerequisite if success is even to be hoped for: We must adjust our methods, our techniques, our actions, and our behavior to get students to adjust theirs. The higher one goes in an organization, the more he or she must be willing to adjust. Likewise, the higher we go in rank, the greater skills we need to be the primary adjustors.

If something isn't getting done or a student behavior isn't being adjusted, we must adjust our actions to see that it does get done. If a student has a "bad attitude," we must adjust our approach to change that negative attitude to a positive one. At times, it may seem our need to adjust is endless. It is. That's why a school needs imaginative, creative, and flexible teachers. It's also the reason we have been chosen to be those teachers. We are supposed to have the skill, self-concept, and personality to lead and manage students. We are supposed to be able to adapt to leading all our students — with their varied motivations and skill levels — to achieve their potential. If we think of ourselves as the primary adjustors in all situations, we have the professional foundation attitude needed to manage kids. If we don't, our students lack a leader. They only have a boss. There is a significant difference.

Accepting and practicing this law is important in relationships with all students, and an absolute in discipline situations. Therefore, the Principle of Management Adjustment is vital to your professional strategic attitude.

PART EIGHT

SHARING VS. IMPOSING TRUTH

Strategic Attitude Rationale: To gain acceptance of beliefs or values, a teacher can and should share his or her truths. However, imposing one's truths upon students is likely to bring rejection rather than acceptance.

In the past, doctors, lawyers, and teachers have held the somewhat Olympian position of being the keepers of special knowledge and truth. From time to time, these truths would be dispensed among the masses, who felt privileged and honored to receive them. Fortunately, that public view has changed. We no longer feel that only certain people in our society have special access to the truth. We all do. And one thing which is being learned about leadership is that nobody can force or impose his or her truths upon others. This is an improvement over previously held public attitudes and beliefs.

You Can Wield Power...Not Truth

A close look at history will reveal that when one group or another has held the reins of power, there was only *one set* of truths. Everyone was expected to abide by the beliefs coming from the group leader. Nothing more could be entered or said. The requirement for living by the established formats of leaders has had several foundations, including familial and political. For instance, if the head of the house believed in certain ways, there was no question that the whole family would have to adopt and conform to these beliefs. The head of the house could insist that his or her truths were the ones to be believed and followed. The rest of the family might differ, and plead that disbelief, compromise, or even immunity should be allowed. Yet, adherence was usually demanded. Herein lies a big lesson for teachers to learn insofar as handling discipline problems is concerned. We need to be careful not to confuse truth-giving with a power play. There's a big difference.

We may be able to control students by wielding power, but no one's mind can be bought unless he or she allows it to be. That's because those beliefs which are truths for us can't be imposed upon students. Our truths can only be shared. Too often, we fail in discipline situations simply because we try to force our truths upon students.

It may come as a surprise to know that we can't even impose truths upon ourselves. We can force ourselves to pretend belief, perhaps because of pressure. But deep within us, seldom, if ever, do we accept what is being imposed upon us as a belief of our own. Until we accept — for ourselves — what is being said, it's not a truth to us. The truths of others don't become ours until we find ourselves living by them. This book, for instance, is my truths. Yet, I can only share these truths. You will only accept my truths in this book when they become yours.

Opinion — Not Truth — Is Rigid

To paraphrase, once we know that we are true to ourselves, we can move on to be true to others. All of our relationships with students are strengthened when we live from the center of our own truths; all our relationships are weakened if we find it necessary to try to live by the truths of people around us. So it is with students.

Many words have been softened and given greater dimension through what we have been learning about people. Truth is one of those words. This is a healthy reality, but we need to take care that certain words don't soften down so much that they have no meaning at all. After all, truth is a dangerous word unless it is handled with respect. That's because it can be transposed into raw power in an instant. This is especially evident in a teacher-pupil relationship. We have no right to talk of truth to students in discipline situations except in our own terms. We can only relate and share our truths — without any strings attached. We cannot tell, demand, or force our truths in absolute ways and expect to get acceptance from misbehaving students. Herein lies a key for getting students to accept what we share with them regarding how they should think, behave, and respond in school. All we need to do is share our truths — and make sure students know we are sharing and not forcing.

If we know that truth is something that keeps changing as we and our world shift, then we can be easy about our use of the word when talking to students. There's one thing truth is not. It's not rigid. When we try to make it rigid, it becomes mere opinion. We should realize the full weight of this possibility and its significance in discipline situations.

Truth is always open to challenge. It can be improved only through openness. These are the things we should keep in mind as we work with young people. Both our ethics and our professionalism should help us to know how to present our truths to students while trying to teach appropriate behavior and striving for acceptance of what we are teaching.

We have opportunities in our classrooms, and especially in discipline situations, to share some things that have become truths for us. And sharing is what we should feel free to do. However, we can't demand that students take on our views or values. We are merely expressing some things that we know to be valid for us which can help our students be successful. It's this fine line that makes the difference between sharing and imposing.

It should always be made clear to students that they have a right to feel however they choose about what we say. In fact, there should be an opportunity in every discipline situation to have good discussion, and we should promote such exchange to improve student learning as well as our own. We may know some truths, but we don't know everything about them. It's always impressive and insightful to hear what a thoughtful student has to add to what we feel we already know.

Summary

Once we can adopt the strategic attitude that permits such freedom, both we and students will come to understand the merit of sharing truths rather than imposing them on each other. It's through this mutual respect for the beliefs of each other that we are positioned to begin the process of teaching and learning from each other. Without such a stance, there are no ingredients for a partnership of any kind. Rather, the openness necessary for meaningful learning has been diminished on both sides of the desk — and raw power has been instilled as a replacement.

Power is a base for wars, not for teaching students acceptable behavior. We can eliminate such barriers simply by telling kids we are sharing rather than telling — and that it's their right to do the accepting. Likewise, we can share those consequences which we think will result if they reject our offering. The choice is ours. This one strategic attitude on our part gives students both the advice and the counseling they need to be responsible for their choices. And our strategic attitude must serve to make children responsible for the choices they make.

PART NINE

THE THEORY OF RIGHT/WRONG CONFLICT

Strategic Attitude Rationale: Right and wrong are immaterial when it comes to solving discipline problems. Therefore, the attitudes, opinions, and beliefs of students cannot be overlooked regardless of the opinion a teacher holds regarding a student attitude, opinion, or belief.

Teachers are concerned with making sound decisions. We do not want to make mistakes. We are very concerned about such things as right and wrong, good and bad, appropriate and inappropriate, correct and incorrect. Unfortunately, our beliefs in these matters often lead us to do and say the wrong things in our leadership role as classroom teachers. In a discipline situation, our beliefs regarding right and wrong can affect our success.

How Students "Think" Is The Real Issue

Right and wrong, good and bad, appropriate and inappropriate, correct and incorrect have meaning to management only insofar as they indicate to teachers what adjustments they must make to change the attitudes and behavior of students. A teacher must never forget that how students ''think'' — what they perceive — is the real issue in any discipline situation. It outweighs all other considerations. That is, it does if teacher leadership is to be accepted and effective in the classroom. Once a teacher knows how students ''think,'' a plan or course of action to enable acceptance can be initiated. Without such consideration, we are likely to ''plow ahead'' with all the right answers and all the wrong questions insofar as students are concerned. When we do, failure rather than success becomes the probability.

Too often, teacher judgments regarding the attitudes, opinions, and beliefs of students keep us from approaching discipline problems successfully, much less solving them. When teachers judge a student's thinking as ''wrong,'' somehow we can and will walk away from that student and problem with the rationalization that ''I'm right — he's wrong.'' Then, we can begin believing that a teacher ''can't'' or ''shouldn't'' do anything about it. This is a management error. What we have forgotten is that right or wrong is insignificant in comparison to relating to students and solving the problem at hand. It is simply not the issue for management.

If your students "think" you're unfair as a teacher — you might as well be. Whether you are or not is insignificant. And you had better meet this problem or it will grow. It does absolutely no good, for instance, for a teacher to prove to colleagues or explain to students why he or she is not unfair. The only positive approach is for teachers to treat the issue.

Summary

To begin changing unacceptable student behavior, we cannot view right and wrong as the primary issue. First, we must know what students "think" or "feel" before we can make the correct decisions regarding how to approach the problem, much less resolve it.

Failure to accept the Theory of Right/Wrong Conflict reflects a failure to accept many other management laws, such as the Law of Positive Reinforcement and the Law of Total Responsibility. Failure to recognize the importance of this theory is often the beginning of misery in a career. But this pitfall can be avoided if teachers will remember to react professionally rather than personally to issues and criticisms, and respond in a positive way to how students "think" or "feel" rather than what a teacher regards as right or wrong.

Accepting and practicing this law is paramount in discipline situations. Therefore, the Theory of Right/Wrong Conflict is vital to your professional strategic attitude.

PART TEN

YOU DON'T HAVE TO UNDERSTAND STUDENTS TO ACCEPT THEM

Strategic Attitude Rationale: To manage discipline problems, a teacher must accept a student even if he or she doesn't understand the student's behavior. Rejection because of a lack of understanding minimizes the possibility of problem solution. Acceptance enhances solutions.

If Anne — whose lifestyle is completely different from our own — does something that we would never do, but we don't walk away from her because of it, we have accepted her. If Tom tells us something that's hard for us to hear, but we can perceive what he said in his terms, then we have understood him. Maybe these examples will help us talk in a professional way about the difference between acceptance and understanding. We need such discussion, for understanding and accepting the behavior and thinking of students can mean the difference between solving discipline problems and living with them.

Having To Understand Everything Would Drain Our Energies As Human Beings

In trying to live our lives, it's not always easy to reach out and include other people in either an accepting or an understanding way. It's possible to go through life practicing neither the concept of understanding nor that of acceptance. Yet, we can hardly call this living. For a professional educator, it's simply not possible to function from such a position and be effective or find any measure of meaningful success in working with any student, much less one who presents a discipline problem.

In addition to a degree of understanding and/or acceptance, we need a third measure called tolerance. However, when we tolerate kids, we're usually gritting our teeth and putting up with them — and that's a long way from accepting and understanding. It may seem difficult continuing to try to draw such distinct lines, but it's much more confusing if we don't. For instance, being able to accept others' differences means being able to take one step to the right and let them pass freely. We need not invest any part of ourselves, nor do they ask us to. We merely have to give them as much breathing room as we expect to have ourselves — nothing more, nothing less.

On the other hand, if we intend to understand someone, it takes both time and some commitment. It requires, at the least, empathetic involvement. Interestingly enough, both acceptance and its wider dimension, understanding, have perfectly valid places in life. However, the burden of thinking we must understand everything would completely drain our energies as human beings. Yet, if we merely accepted without ever going further, the resulting distortions of a relationship would end up being as burdensome as any other one-sidedness which could be introduced.

As Teachers, We Don't Need To Understand A Child's Home Life...But We Must Accept It

Teachers should practice both concepts with equal zeal. And we should discard thinking in terms of tolerance — except on the rarest of occasions when all else fails. Then, we should be tolerant.

As teachers, we need to remember that children bring to school the lifestyles, beliefs, behaviors, manners, and even the hang-ups of those with whom they live. Their ways of functioning will match our own in some respects — and not at all in others. This is a point at which some teachers become high-and-mighty moralists. They don't mean to be, but they know that the way they think and live is the right way. If we feel this way, our ability to accept hasn't been very extensively developed. As a result, our relationships with many students may be scrambled and we may have trouble understanding or accepting anything. Rather, we will have to survive through tolerance. This is a hard way to live and leads to a great deal of stress.

This is a situation in which acceptance is in order, but understanding doesn't need to be included — except as a secondary thought. For instance, it's important that we accept that children act differently because of their diverse home lives. However, as their teachers, we don't need to make a big effort to understand why that home life is the way it is. It's enough to accept the fact that it is that way. If we see a home environment and conclude that a certain child is uncomfortable as a member of the family, and this is reflected in the child's school work, then it's our duty to try to understand the child's feelings and to keep an eye on the dimensions of his or her upset. It will be through our empathy and concern that we can move past acceptance and offer our understanding.

Realize that people often have trouble balancing the weights of these two concepts. But experience and thoughtfulness are our best teachers. Given time and thought, we don't have to wonder which strategic attitude would be best if we want to be successful — in handling discipline problems as well as in maintaining our own mental health.

Without question, our lives can be improved through acceptance. Students will know almost immediately on entering our room whether or not we accept them. If they feel that we do, then their confidence is elevated to a point at which they can also know that they can depend upon our understanding them. From this grows a mutuality of respect which can be the basis for all else that follows — including the handling of misbehavior.

Summary

With this one strategic attitude, we can function without frustration or guilt because we don't have to understand children to accept them. Neither do we have to like what we accept. After all, children may not understand why we are teachers, but they still accept us as their teachers. Acceptance is not judgmental. Neither is it approving or disapproving. Understanding is a cognitive behavior, while acceptance is an affective behavior. One comes from the head and the other from the heart. To be a happy as well as successful teacher, one needs to be led by both. That's why adopting the strategic attitude of acceptance can be so beneficial in handling all students — especially discipline problems. And without such a strategic attitude, students who are discipline problems may never let us get close enough to them to effect any changes in behavior. Herein lies our task — changing behavior. Without acceptance of the reason, this may not be possible.

PART ELEVEN

DISCIPLINE CAN'T BE LEGISLATED FROM THE OFFICE

Strategic Attitude Rationale: Once students are in the classroom, office and administrator influence is present, but office control is not. In a classroom, good discipline is the responsibility of the teacher and results from teacher skill, not administrative rules.

The subject of discipline probably receives more teacher attention and causes more teacher concern than any other single school responsibility. We, as teachers, tend to have firm convictions regarding the "hows, whys, and whens" of good discipline. Yet, the big area of discipline disagreement among educators is who should discipline and who is responsible for discipline in a school. This reality affects our professional strategic attitude and, therefore, affects our success as individuals and as a staff.

Different Opinions

Some teachers firmly believe that discipline is not primarily a teacher responsibility. Many teachers are convinced that discipline is the total responsibility of the administration. They will argue that any problem that occurs in a classroom or the halls can be directly related to an office failure and should, without reservation, be handled by the office. They say that any child who is a classroom disturbance should be sent immediately to the office and kept there until proper behavior can be guaranteed by student and administrator alike. Many will add that student reentry to class should be accompanied by teacher approval.

It's true that administrators do play a big role in the discipline of a good school. But one thing is certain: Discipline can't be legislated from the office.

What The Office Can Do

The office can suspend, of course. It can even recommend expulsion. However, the primary function of the office is to establish the guidelines for student behavior. It can set the standards for expected conduct and communicate these standards to students through handbooks, announcements, parent newsletters, and other communicative devices. Administrators can give discipline codes the fairness, objectivity, uniformity, and continuity needed by both students and teachers in a school. They can support teacher action with a child and parents, and they can correct teacher misaction. Administrators can also give guidance and assistance in helping teachers become more proficient in avoiding and eliminating discipline problems in their classrooms. That's what administrators are for — to assist teachers in meeting their responsibilities. However, that's about as much as any administrator can do to help an individual teacher correct discipline problems.

Once students are with their teacher in a classroom, discipline is a personal matter between the teacher and the student or students. Office influence is present, but office control is not. Never believe for one minute that office influence will be enough to control a class. It will not. And the teacher who attempts to use office influence as a threat will find about as much success as the mother who says, "I'll tell your father when he gets home." That's why a teacher must have an awareness that good discipline comes out of mutual respect, which grows out of trust. And this, in turn, results from the viable close interaction between teacher and student that has nothing to do with the office.

In some ways, a teacher's situation is similar to that of a babysitter who has been entrusted with supervision of children during their parents' absence. Parents may talk to their children before they leave regarding the guidelines for behavior in their absence. They can even warn their children about punishment and, in fact, administer severe punishment when children do misbehave. They can counsel the babysitter with advice and instructions and offer suggestions regarding the best way to achieve success with their children. However, once the parents leave the house, responsibility for the children's behavior belongs only to the sitter. If a sitter cannot manage the children, regardless of parent action following their return, the chances are the babysitter will have the same problem each time he or she works. Only when the babysitter learns to handle the problem will it be solved.

Parents do have a responsibility to the babysitter. And, yes, care of the children is the responsibility of both. Yet the fact remains, the sitter has the authority and responsibility for the care and behavior of the children and only the sitter can gain control of the situation. One thing is certain: As long as the babysitter blames the parents for the failure experienced and until the babysitter can accept the responsibility for the situation, any problem will continue. The same is true for a teacher.

Summary

If all the teachers in a school can't control their students, then the administration has, indeed, failed. The administrators have fallen short in providing reasonable standards and usable guidelines for teachers and students. They have not communicated or enforced standards so as to create a climate of order necessary for teacher instruction and student learning. However, we should recognize that if the majority of teachers are establishing and maintaining standards of good conduct while a few are not, then the fault lies with these teachers themselves.

The office is, without reservation, an influence — but not the control — for discipline in a classroom. Discipline in a school is only as effective as are the teachers as individuals, and the staff as a whole, in enforcing the office guidelines with fairness, uniformity, and consistency. The primary purpose of discipline is teaching self-discipline. Achieving self-discipline is daily learning that must be experienced in the classroom along with academics in order for children to prepare for a meaningful life. It can be taught only by people who touch the lives of young people daily with expectations of good conduct and enforcement of appropriate standards. Office legislation does not have this direct personal contact — only the teacher does. To be a successful disciplinarian, a teacher must accept this concept as a part of the professional strategic attitude.

PART TWELVE

YOU CAN'T HAVE RULES FOR EVERYTHING

Strategic Attitude Rationale: The need for rules is unquestionable. However, rules can cause both inflexibility for teachers and injustice for students. The less need there is to make a rule, the greater opportunity there is for flexibility and fairness.

Those of us in teaching are usually good organizers. We are planners. We like to have guidelines for students because we need them. After all, we teach in a room full of students doing a wide variety of tasks. That's why we are prone to favor specific rules and regulations that govern the behavior of students — and punish their misbehavior. We might even want standard operating procedures which could be applied to all activities and all places in the school, including the hall, playground, cafeteria, gym, auditorium, and classroom.

There is no doubt that rules and regulations are necessary in a school. There is also no question that standard operating procedures can be valuable behavioral and performance aids. There is, however, a question regarding the number and scope of rules we should adopt for both. That's why we need to understand the purpose of rules and procedures and how they affect our relationships with students and staff alike.

The Purpose Of Rules

School rules and standard procedures do facilitate general understanding. They do promote security and a smoothly running school. Certainly, none can deny that rules facilitate group learning and offer protection to the individual as well as the group. Standard procedures are aids in control, direction, time management, task completion, and evaluation of students. These are some of the reasons we have rules and standard procedures in the first place.

However, our need for rules can cause inflexibility. When rules are absolutes, they can also cause us to perpetuate injustice. And this is vital because a school and classroom must be a "fair and just" place for students. If it isn't, we teach unfairness and injustice and these characteristics will destroy student confidence in us and in schools. Worse, they may be perpetuated by students. Then, learning self-discipline and other actions necessary for good behavior is impossible. That's why the *limitations* as well as the merits of rules and standard procedures should be understood by teachers. In truth, if we can reduce the need for absolute rules and standard operating procedures in administering a classroom or a school, we allow ourselves more flexibility to be fair and position ourselves to make more sound decisions. That's a fact.

The purpose of both rules and standard operating procedures in a school is to create desired patterns of behavior. It is not to create desired absolutes. As teachers, we need to think about this reality — or the purpose of rules and procedures may get confused with the punishments for breaking them. We may find ourselves in constant turmoil with students and colleagues because of rules and punishments. To ask administrators to issue fixed punishments in every instance is to demand that they be both unfair and unwise.

Making Allowances

In many ways, the needs and desires of the faculty dictate the rules which are made in a school. It's easy to understand why. Administrators simply respond to staff needs and pressure. That's precisely why teacher attitudes regarding rules, procedures, and the enforcing of rules are so vitally important in a school.

When standard operating procedures for everything are a must, standards are usually lowered rather than raised. They have to be — for we can't make rules which the vast majority can't handle. In the classroom, standard procedures usually lower expectations for behavior and achievement. That's why we must realize that rules and standard procedures can limit productivity, curtail motivation, and hinder the individual decision-making process.

Remember, what standard procedures do for group control, they do against individual initiative and creative thinking. What standard procedures do for group understanding, they do against individual productivity. Regulations and standard procedures work best for simple, routine tasks — not creative ones. Most important, guidelines should never be mixed with enforcement. When they are, we are never able to make allowances when a rule is broken. Rather, we may be forced into frequent injustice by our inflexibility.

As teachers, we should never be in a position in which we must act in the best interests of a rule rather than the best interests of a person. If we do, we may act unfairly and unwisely. And we can't get kids to adjust their behavior if we are regarded as unfair. The teacher must establish a climate in the classroom which is fair, just, and caring. Too often, our own rules prevent us from being fair or caring because we have to show more care for a rule than for a child. Remember, if extenuating circumstances count in a court of law, they must count in our classrooms.

Summary

We can't have rules for everything in a school or a classroom. Neither can we fix specific punishments and insist upon absolutes for every violation. That is, we can't if we want to do what is best for students.

If we insist on absolute rules with absolute penalties, we need to ask ourselves why we do. If the purpose of our rules is to create a desired behavior pattern, why should punishment be added if a lesson has been learned already? If students have learned from an error, should we not forget about punishment? If the counseling efforts of colleagues and administrators have been successful, should we not be satisfied and admit the success of our efforts? Of course we should.

The less we are compelled to establish absolute rules for everything, the more room we have to operate as professional educators. The less we must follow standard procedures, the more we are positioned to be fair and sensible in our relationships with students and each other. On the other hand, when we are locked into absolutes, we are forced to be police officers rather than educators. Then, our guidelines may work more against us than they do for us. That's why we should allow ourselves flexibility by not insisting that administrators make rules for everything. In truth, we need but one general rule in the classroom: No disrespect for people or property, including oneself. This one rule gives students the necessary guidelines and gives us the flexibility to discipline in positive ways. When we adopt this professional strategic attitude, we are best positioned to teach appropriate behavior as well as to solve discipline problems in a class and in a school.

PART THIRTEEN

THE KIDS WHO NEED US THE MOST...

Strategic Attitude Rationale: The children who need teachers the most and are often the most influenced by teachers are those who misbehave — and even show disregard for school — most frequently.

Most of the time we feel very good about what we are doing as educators. If we didn't, we wouldn't choose to continue being teachers. Yet, sometimes we aren't quite certain how effective we are — especially with certain students. Those students who don't want to learn, who skip class, and who don't seem to care about us or anything we are trying to do cause us to have grave doubts. Unfortunately, we don't always think we are an influential part of their lives. Yet, a closer look might tell us a different story. We just may be more important in the lives of these students than we ever dared dream.

A Reality

The plain truth is that teachers can be totally wrong about their influence and effectiveness with discipline problems. That's because students don't always show us how important we are to them. And there's reason to believe that we are, and that we become even more significant to some students as the years pass and they become adults.

It may seem that many of the lessons we teach children aren't being absorbed. They are, but some lessons may not "take" until much later. That's why we must be careful about judging today's efforts. If we aren't, we may give up on some students when we shouldn't.

In truth, if we come right to the heart of the matter, teachers often want to be with those students who need them the least. And this is understandable. After all, we want to teach today. It's normal to like and relate to good students easily. It's normal to prefer working with the caring and serious learners. They make our days. This may not be true of the lazy, tardy, absent, or disinterested students who are always a discipline problem of some kind. Yet, school may be a big, if not the biggest, part of the lives of these students. In fact, their teachers and school experiences may remain with these students longer and more forcefully than they do with students who excel.

After all, which students show up on elementary playgrounds after they have been promoted to junior high? Which ones do we see on streets in front of junior highs and middle schools after they are in high school? Which people attend every high school athletic event after graduation? Which ones never miss a class reunion or always remember our names long after we have had them in class? Which former pupils speak fondly of us, hoping we will remember them? And, which ones come to see us after they graduate? More often than not, it's those students we couldn't keep in class when we had them — those who seemed most disinterested and uninvolved at the time. It's those students we thought cared the least about us and school. But they did care. We were influential — very influential — with these students. Time and experience have proven this to be true.

A Lesson To Be Learned

We can learn a valuable lesson because of this reality. As classroom teachers, we are the most vital element in the learning process. And we are always teachers, even when we sometimes think we are not. That's why our responsibility to reach students must never lessen. Adopting this strategic attitude is paramount to our short- and long-term success as well as to our fulfillment in teaching.

Therefore, if we will remind ourselves constantly that the students who need us the most may be the ones we want to be with the least, we may change our professional strategic attitude. We may also alter our interest in students who behave inappropriately, as well as our feelings and actions toward them. We can, if we resolve never to quit and never to ignore any student. If we remember that learning — including learning to behave appropriately — has no starting or shut-off point, we will never close any doors. Rather, we will make sure that all students are constantly reminded that opportunity is always waiting. And we will make sure that students are *never* told that they "are no good" or "will never amount to anything." To adopt a positive strategic stance, it may help to look at our former pupils who, though unsuccessful in school, are now highly successful adults. Then, we might all realize that the vast majority of students will do very well, even those we thought might not.

That's why we need to give students the opportunity to have our unconditional friendship. By responding in professional ways, we keep the door open for possible change whenever it's happening. It might be easier to stay turned on to the possibilities if we remember that our students are only children, and they simply can't handle any of our actions which come out of rejection. We must always tell students when they are doing things they shouldn't, of course. We must hold firm to teaching them as we know they should be taught. However, we must be careful about rejection because no matter how wrong students are or how bad their behavior, they still need us if a turnaround is to be possible *while* they are still in school.

Summary

We often can't judge accurately the effectiveness of our teaching efforts on any given day. The plain truth is that we may or may not ever really know how significant we are in the lives of students on any one given day. That's why we must always be teachers in the true sense of the word. This means in the classroom, halls, playgrounds, streets, and even restrooms.

The joys and rewards teachers receive come in unusual as well as usual ways. They come from expected and unexpected places. And the rewards come from all students. From those who are successful learners, the benefits are usually immediate. From those who are less than we would like them to be at the moment, we may not know until years later, if at all, that we were effective. Regardless, we need to remember that our lessons are "taking" for most of those we teach. Most students will grow up to be responsible adults who go to work, pay their bills, and try to rear their own children in acceptable, loving ways. And many of these ways they learned from us, as well as from other adults in their lives.

If we give all students our best effort, the future holds its best chance for them. And if we don't give up or quit, many of those we teach may come to know much more quickly how important we were in their lives. As we all know, the sooner students make this discovery, the sooner they can experience the rewards of learning. This fact alone should be all the incentive we need to teach all students — even those who act as if they don't want us.

Adopting this professional strategic attitude can make us more successful in discipline situations. It can also help our mental health as we strive to be good teachers. If we refuse this strategic attitude, we may experience needless misery as teachers.

PART FOURTEEN

THE LAW OF FILTERED INFORMATION

Strategic Attitude Rationale: The more power and influence a teacher possesses, the more information received from students will be filtered.

"I want the whole truth ..."

"Who is responsible for this?"

"Tell me everything that you did ..."

We ask students to tell us the whole truth many times when they or someone else misbehaves. And we expect complete answers. More often than we might suspect, we don't get total answers. We get partial ones. Sometimes big parts are left out of the answers given us regarding who did what and why. We may be disappointed. We may even think students can't be trusted. After all, our expectations of young people are high. And the least they can do is own up to what they did and tell the truth when asked. When we don't get the whole truth, we may alter our opinion of a child or even a whole class. We shouldn't. Such behavior is quite normal. There's no need to be disappointed or to think students aren't cooperating, are acting against us, or are being untrustworthy. They are simply exhibiting normal behavior. That's why we need to understand the "whys" behind such student behavior, and know what to do about them as professional teachers. Such understanding can help our strategic attitude.

The Whys

The Law of Filtered Information fully explains why students don't tell the whole truth in some situations. This law states that information received from students by a person in a position of authority is filtered, by either omission or distortion, if that information reflects negatively upon the person(s) doing the telling. This is true whether the leader is a general in an army, a school administrator, or a teacher — and whether subordinates are soldiers, teachers, or students. This law contains a vital piece of knowledge for anyone in a leadership position such as teaching. Without it, wrong conclusions can be reached, and the resulting actions taken may make bad situations worse.

There are many reasons why some consider this law to be an absolute. Often, people in subordinate positions can temporarily rationalize their actions because of a need for self-preservation. Students are not the exception. That's why they may not tell us everything in problem situations. Self-protection keeps them from telling the whole truth. In addition, when dealing with the boss, almost all people consciously make three assumptions which may or may not be true.

The Three Assumptions

First, people feel that it's not their responsibility to tell someone in authority something that would cause their own judgment, competency, or actions to be revealed in an unfavorable light. In truth, they may not even think the person in authority has the right to ask them to do so. This doesn't mean they will lie. It simply means they may omit some very important facts. This assumption is reinforced regarding what students tell teachers. After all, if they tell, they may end up getting disapproval from teachers and classmates alike.

Second, it's automatically assumed that the person in authority has more information than he or she is revealing. Therefore, students may assume that they're expected to provide only a part of the information a teacher is requesting. For instance, if a teacher is asking who stole something, students honestly believe the teacher has talked to others before talking to them. This assumption allows students to rationalize not answering questions fully.

Finally, it's assumed that teachers are asking questions only to confirm information that they already know. This assumption is often reinforced when teachers act superior or pretend to know more than they do. More important, students are apt to believe that teachers should know or should have a very good idea regarding a matter — and if teachers say they don't, students believe that teachers are being dishonest with them.

Summary

The Law of Filtered Information contains a vital lesson for every teacher. It gives us a foundation in human behavior needed for problem situations. That's why we can never forget that students usually assume we know what's going on. It's taken for granted that we have vast sources of information which are not available to them. This assumption makes the job of gaining accurate information more difficult, which in turn makes problem solving more difficult because we need information to make good decisions. Herein lies the danger of not learning the lesson taught by the Law of Filtered Information.

In our search for accurate information, we may make some very serious mistakes. We may forget that because of their humanness, kids may be omitting necessary facts when they are answering our questions. We need to realize that they are acting to satisfy their need for security rather than against us personally. So we had better not call them liars. We'd better be careful about saying and doing things that make them feel less secure with us. And we need to remember that all the assumptions made by students in a given situation are temporary — not permanent. So if we make fewer demands in problem situations, we may find we gain more information with each passing minute. Above all, we must never use one student or a small group of students as a source for the whole of our information. If we do, our information about everything is limited. And, as the law teaches, if the student from whom we seek information is involved in the issue or experiencing peer pressure, our information may be worthless — and the rest of our students will know it.

If we expect our students to disappoint us in discipline situations, many surely will. But they may disappoint us not because of a character flaw, but because of their humanness. However, it is they who should really be disappointed in us. After all, students should be able to expect us to understand our leadership responsibility, the circumstances involved in a situation, and human behavior and problem solving. They should also be able to count on us not to make every problem a bigger one. If we understand the Law of Filtered Information and make it a part of our strategic attitude in problem situations, we won't disappoint students and won't be disappointed ourselves.

CHAPTER 3

STRATEGIC POSITION

PART ONE

PROFESSIONAL STRATEGIC POSITION

Our desires as educators are simple and direct. We want to teach and we want our students to learn. And we want as few problems as possible in the process. In truth, however, without our being *strategically positioned* to teach, none of these three teacher desires may be possible. The question is: What do we intend to do to *position ourselves* for teaching and learning — as well as for relating to and solving discipline problems? I say that because we often worry so much about positioning ourselves to establish order and control that we sacrifice everything else in the process. There's no doubt that we need order and control in the classroom, but we also need the climate and relationship necessary for teaching and learning.

How You Decide To Position Yourself As A Teacher Is A Vital Decision

Without reservation, how you decide to position yourself as a teacher is the most important decision you will ever make in the classroom. You can position yourself as a learning leader or as the boss. You can position yourself as helper or judge, friend or enemy, teacher or buddy. You can position yourself as the person who solves problems — or as the one who doesn't want problems or the people who have them. You can position yourself to make the most of individual student strengths and potentials — or capitulate to the weakness of every child. Likewise, you can position yourself to lead only because it's your job — or because of your professional commitment to students. Positioning is everything in management. Management not positioned to lead cannot lead.

Sometimes we inadvertently position ourselves incorrectly. We begin contact with students by stating all our rules, regulations, and requirements. We may even tell students what will happen if they violate our rules. We may choose this position because we are worried about possible problems rather than enthusiastic about the possibilities. Likewise, instead of being confident of student success, we're fearful that students can't or won't do the work. Yet, our *chosen* strategic position determines whether we say to students, "This course or test is going to be hard," or "Don't worry; I'm here to help you all do well." If we use the first position and some children have difficulty, we should know why. Our positioning told them what to expect. Our stance may even have told students not to see us about problems because problems should be expected.

Remember, positioning is everything in management. And make no mistake, a teacher is management in the classroom. Without an attitude and a plan that give students success, a teacher is not strategically positioned to teach academics or appropriate behavior. Neither are students positioned to expect to be successful, or reasonably successful, learners.

Making Your Students A Promise

The second most important decision you make concerns what you should *promise* your students. A promise is not a threat, ultimatum, or slogan. It's a benefit. Sometimes, we promise students nothing. In fact, we may ask children to make us promises that they will be quiet, listen, behave, and work hard, before they can expect anything from us.

Yet, without a teacher promise, it's unlikely that students will readily accept and follow our leadership. And that's what teaching appropriate behavior is: leadership.

It pays to promise your students that you can and will help them to be successful. This is the best promise you can make in order to keep a position of leadership with all students in the classroom, especially those who are discipline problems. It's easy to see why.

Young people want to be successful. Some expect to be, and others have lost their expectations. Those who act uninterested or cause problems often do so because they feel they can't succeed in school — and for good reason. They have failed in the past. Unfortunately, teachers in the past may have told them or proved to them that they weren't smart or didn't measure up. This is a mistake we can never make if we want to be strategically positioned to teach academics or behavior. With the promise of our help and their own efforts, students must be able to both anticipate and experience success — or they'll quit. That's because most students, including good students, honestly feel that they can't do school work successfully alone — they need the help of their teacher.

Positive, Constructive Ideas

Therefore, our two most important decisions as teachers have to do with our *positioning* in the classroom and the *promise* we make to students. Then, we must deliver the benefits promised. Too many teachers promise nothing, then can't understand why students won't follow — and will even fight — their leadership. In addition, unless our strategic position in the classroom is built upon positive ideas for helping students achieve success in school, our efforts will have no effect on students. It takes constructive ideas to jolt some kids out of their indifference — to make them notice and accept their misdeeds, and take action to follow teacher guidance.

A teacher must never forget that nobody is ever bored into following leadership. Being a leader requires being positioned to lead. And positioning precedes action. Too many teachers have a positioning style that is impersonal, detached, cold — and dull. Leadership without involvement is all of these negatives. It pays to be positioned for involvement with your students. Talk to them like human beings. Care about them and charm them. Make them hungry to improve. Get them to participate in their own successes, show them how to win, and you'll find leading easier. Without professional strategic positions which are personal and caring, a teacher is not very apt to find success in managing children who have discipline problems.

Summary

The term "learning leader" denotes that students and teacher are learning together. This means that adopting a superior stance is never in order. We must, however, by the nature of the school experience, be both helpers and evaluators, of course. Evaluating is an inescapable responsibility that comes with the job. However, the message must be, "I'm here to help you learn. The evaluation will be a measure of how well *we both have succeeded.*"

Without taking this professional strategic position, we are denied the privilege of making students the most important of all promises — that we will help them learn and be successful. This promise is the encouragement students need to accept their role in the classroom. Once they believe they can succeed, we can teach. That's why the classroom is not a place for negatives. A club will not pull young people toward you, and is guaranteed to push behavior problems beyond the reach of your influence.

As adults, when we are in a problem situation, we look for concerned and caring people to help us adjust to that situation. So do students. They do not need tough, distant, and hard-nosed adults as advocates. Rather, they need caring teachers who are willing to promise them help — and then make good on their promise. Therefore, this must be your strategic position if you intend to manage learning and behavior.

PART TWO

DISCIPLINE IS NOT A NEGATIVE

Strategic Position Rationale: Discipline is a positive force in the lives of students. Yet, only after we teach children who exhibit inappropriate behavior the proper way to behave do they have a chance to control and/or change their behavior.

Often, discipline is looked upon as a negative part of teaching. It's often a negative part of our relationships with students as well. Worse, many teachers feel helpless to effect behavior change, and believe the majority of student behavior is actually irreversible.

We may never solve all our discipline problems. Yet, if we can cut down on the number of students regarded as discipline problems as well as the number of times certain students misbehave, we shall be guaranteed a better teaching year. Before we begin, however, we need to adopt a positive attitude toward discipline so that our professional strategic position toward discipline facilitates success rather than failure.

Discipline Involves More Than Student Behavior

Most often, we think of discipline in terms of correcting student misbehavior or in relation to students possessing self-discipline. The latter may include behavior as well as such student characteristics as organization, will power, consideration, and persistence. In truth, however, the two aspects of discipline can't be mixed. Only after we teach children who exhibit inappropriate behavior the proper way to behave do they have a chance to control and change their misbehavior. Only after this teacher action can we teach students to develop other vital personal disciplines. Remember, refined discipline goes beyond good behavior. It's having one's life under control. To teach this level of discipline, we must — without reservation — first be highly disciplined ourselves.

Our professional strategic position is shaped from our attitudes toward discipline. That's why we first need to accept the reality that "discipline" is a positive word. Discipline is also an individual opportunity. And it goes without saying that teaching students discipline — in all aspects of life — is vital to student success. Without discipline, little opportunity for success lies ahead for anyone, including students.

If we look upon discipline as a negative aspect of teaching, our attitude can affect our strategic skills. Too often, unfortunately, we don't really view discipline as a part of our teaching responsibility. It is. Worse, if our strategic stance toward discipline is not positive, we tune out some kids. As a result, these students may feel "forced out" of the classroom, the school situation, and the desire to behave in acceptable ways for self-gain. Then, the possibilities for them to develop positive discipline characteristics are diminished.

Two Teacher Guides: The Principle Of Adjustment And The Law Of Positive Reinforcement

It's a fact: Students who habitually misbehave usually haven't been taught proper behavior or the personal value of behaving appropriately.

To teach acceptable behavior, we must first back up — usually in terms of what students have already learned about acceptable behavior by a certain age. Just as some children are academically behind their classmates, others lag in learning proper behavior. In addition, some kids only get recognized and accepted by peers for misbehaving. Therefore, it is not safe for them to behave.

In teaching students how to be self-disciplined, you simply must practice the management principle of adjustment. Remember, this principle reveals that the only way you can change student behavior is to adjust your own first. Therefore, when it comes to teaching self-discipline, you need to adjust your techniques to fit the child you are teaching. In the process, you must always tell young people what you're going to teach them about discipline — and why. And your explanation of why must include the personal benefits, values, and rewards of being disciplined.

Finally, you must accept the fact that without positive reinforcement from teachers, negative attitudes and behaviors toward being disciplined may dominate student action. Remember, two negatives never mix here. If students are behaving badly and you become the second negative in their lives, all is lost. That's why you must take a professional look at discipline. You must view it as a potential teaching opportunity. Understand, too, that there are some basic preventers of bad student behavior. These include starting class on time, being in the room early, making expectations clear, being considerate, and helping students be successful. In addition, you must recognize that you can make allowances for variations in student behavior — if doing so doesn't stop the teaching flow in the classroom.

Summary

We can reject behavior, but we can't reject students as people and expect to change behavior. In teaching self-discipline, therefore, the "reasoning technique" is exceptionally successful. Its value must never be overlooked.

With this technique, we simply teach students to classify the importance of things that enter their lives. We counsel them to rate everything in terms of what it can mean to them by putting their actions on a plus and minus basis — including the pluses and minuses which cause them to lose their control. Then, we can ask them to answer, "How much good did it do not to opt for proper behavior?" The reason this technique works is that it's individualized, works from the thinking and feeling of each student, and allows students to develop an awareness of self-discipline and establish values — as well as think and decide for themselves. This is in contrast to what students usually get — somebody else deciding for them what they should do and why.

When we take time to look toward preventive discipline, it's time apart from academics. We may feel this is not our job. Worse, we may feel it's a waste of time. It's not. Rather, it's an opportunity which may, indeed, help students with their academic skills. That's why we must acquire the skills of teaching proper behavior and self-discipline — and recognize that such a strategic position is an important part of being a successful teacher.

PART THREE

THE FOUR RELATIONSHIPS OF STUDENTS

Strategic Position Rationale: Every student has four relationships in the classroom; these relationships are themselves interrelated and cannot be dealt with separately.

The formulation of appropriate behavior for a student in a school is, without doubt, the result of at least four relationships. They are:

- Student and Himself/Herself
- Student and Teacher
- Student and Classroom Activities
- Student and Peers

As a primary instrument for the development and fulfillment of these relationships, a teacher can never forget — even for a moment — that the student is the common element in all of them. Too, these relationships cannot be separated, for they are interrelated — and this must be the focus for teacher emphasis, especially in discipline situations. The real question is, "How does a classroom teacher relate to students as they function within these four relationships?"

The Student And Himself/Herself

First, a teacher can best begin helping a child by not "writing the child off" because of behavior, achievement, or personality. Too often, we "size up" kids on the first day of school or sometime during the year. How often have you heard someone say, "I've got his number"? Impossible! When we do this, we have stepped out of the arena of diagnosticians to become prejudgers. This is a mistake for teacher and child alike.

Never forget that a student comes to the classroom having had five to eighteen years to think about who he or she is, what he or she is, and what he or she wants to be. Our role as teachers is not to view students as we see them ourselves. Rather, it is to view them as they see themselves. This is the key to understanding behavior. It is the only strategic position that allows a teacher to detect truth.

When we "size up" students, and then proceed, we usually proceed in the wrong direction. Failure to view a child as the child sees himself or herself often causes teachers to put the student in positions, within each of the four relationships, that the student can't deal with. The most drastic example of this mistake is the student who displays an extreme change in behavior and may even do something dishonest that shocks us. How many times have you heard someone say, "Joan was such a nice girl. She had everything going for her. What happened?" Well, one thing happened for sure. Somebody did not see Joan as she saw herself. Had someone been alert enough to recognize how Joan felt about herself, maybe "what happened" wouldn't have happened.

There are students sitting in classrooms — many of whom are discipline problems — whom we don't know. If we want to change their behavior, it's time to begin finding out how they view themselves. Then, and only then, can what we do to change their behavior have any real meaning.

Student-Teacher Relationship

Teachers must elevate their thinking regarding the student-teacher relationship. Many teachers' thoughts include, "How can I get along with students, and how can students get along with me?" Needless to say, however, the emphasis is generally on the latter.

Never overlook the fact that students do not necessarily come to class liking the teacher or vice versa. But all students do enter class, consciously or subconsciously, looking for help and wanting, hoping, or wishing to be successful. Thus, a teacher's responsibility is to give help and cause children to be successful in class. Problems for teachers come when, for one reason or another, they deny help or can't help a child be successful. And there are many ways to deny a child the student-teacher relationship which is necessary for sound mental health. Usually we deny students this relationship by what we are or are not doing, such as judging them slow, ignoring their questions, overlooking their failures, or classifying their interests as trivial. Teachers need only to review their grade book name by name to see how they are affecting the student-teacher relationship of each child entrusted to their care. One thing is certain according to all research, including that of Leon Lessinger. Three things are needed to be a successful person. First, one must feel successful. Second, one must believe that others feel he or she is successful. Third, one must have ownership. The teacher plays a vital role in all three of these necessities. However, the sense of ownership ties everything together. That's why children must have input into what we are trying to teach them. And we can give ownership by making it a student's book, a student's work, and a student's responsibility. Any time we deny ownership in a class, we increase the possibility of misbehavior.

Student And Curriculum Activities

This is the student relationship we know best. Yet, we often think of the class and the curriculum rather than the student and the curriculum. Without doubt, curriculum activities place some students in an impossible situation. This is most obvious on the secondary level. Math, for instance, may be an overwhelmingly difficult experience for some students, but without it they know they cannot graduate. Therefore, some students struggle, often against almost insurmountable odds, and become more and more frustrated when no provision is made within the curriculum for them as individuals.

If you have difficulty accepting the need for flexibility in class requirements, examine some of the students in your school who are regarded as failures. You'll find that at some point most of these students excelled in some areas and with some teachers. Yet, if you trace their history, you can often find a curriculum problem that caused a whole chain of events that spelled school trouble. A teacher must always be aware of the academic relationship in a child's life. The relationship of student and curriculum activities can be the problem. Once this is detected, flexible in-class requirements, as well as teacher approach and attitude, can provide this student with fulfillment rather than frustration.

Student And Peers

In one way or another, everybody needs somebody. The child who cannot relate to his or her peers is in trouble — and will generally cause trouble in a class. There is much a teacher can do for a student to fulfill the need for peer relationships. We deny it most, though, by our classroom structure. The lecture situation does absolutely nothing to help students with developing peer relationships. Neither does the ''stand up, sit down, raise your hand, and I'll recognize you'' type of teacher. Here, the student has no opportunity to develop any of his or her four relationships.

Summary

The teacher is the primary instrument in the creation of good mental health and, therefore, good discipline in the classroom. And climate is, without reservation, vital in determining the well-being of students as well as the success of a teacher. Each student has at least four relationships in a classroom. All four relationships of students are interrelated. In every situation, a teacher cannot look at one without also looking at the other three.

In most cases that baffle a teacher, one of three mistakes has been made.

Often, the teacher has "figured out" the student without really looking at the student and his or her four relationships — individually. Second, a teacher may look at one facet without awareness of the other three and their importance. Third, a teacher may deny students these relationships. When we do these things, we have arrived at all our answers without asking the right questions. The chance of children becoming discipline problems has increased, because kids think that they aren't successful and that others (including the teacher) don't regard them as successful, and because some measure of ownership has been denied them. In this case, teachers are likely to think in terms of "my room, my class, my books, my course, and my day." Remember, without giving kids ownership, it is difficult to teach responsibility and self-discipline. That's why understanding these four relationships must be a foundation of your professional strategic position if you are to be effective in discipline situations.

PART FOUR

PROCTOR'S SPIRAL OF FUTILITY

Strategic Position Rationale: Futility is not one condition, but a seven-step process which is reversible. However, improvement occurs in the same order of steps and, therefore, a child must be helped back through the spiral, or regression will occur.

We've all seen young people go from bad to worse. We watch the despair as they seem to give up. If we could do something, we would. Fortunately, we can. That's why being aware of Proctor's Spiral of Futility is vitally important to teachers when it comes to helping students behave. It reveals the stages some children go through — beginning with rejection and ending with crime and violence. Of paramount significance, however, is the fact that the spiral can be reversed with one major intervention. All we need to do is determine where children are in the downward spiral and intervene. We can even seek the help of others when we do. It is vital that we position ourselves strategically in order to take action.

Rejection Is The Beginning

The spiral of futility begins with an awareness or feeling of *rejection.* Rejection may be real or imaginary — at home, with peers, or with teachers. After all, rejection may come from many sources. This feeling of rejection can begin in young people when others doubt their word, they can't do certain tasks satisfactorily, they aren't chosen or considered in activities, or they experience low expectations at home or at school. Regardless, a feeling of rejection is the beginning.

Rejection is followed by *voluntary or involuntary isolation.* Young people in this stage move away from others. They may not have friends in school, or may spend a lot of time in their rooms alone. If one of these students appears to have a friend, both may be experiencing isolation and feeling alone — even when they're together.

These kids move from isolation to the position of *insularity* — the condition of being an "island." They become narrow-minded and prejudiced against popular students. They also oppose accepted beliefs and authority. They begin to feel that nobody cares — and as a result withdraw even further.

At this point, *hostility* surfaces. They become unfriendly and openly disagreeable. In many ways, they are at war. They become fighters. They take on hateful characteristics and will fight anyone — just to hurt. They also destroy property — just to get even. They hurt parents by misbehaving, bringing discredit, and destroying family property. Suddenly, they find they feel good only when they hurt someone.

Even The Final Stage Is Reversible

Hostility is followed by a *withdrawal from success symbols.* These students will openly refuse to do school work, will become disruptive on purpose, and start talking back to parents and teachers alike. In fact, the activities they choose are those that represent everything disapproved of at home and at school. They will, indeed, reject any idea, belief, or institution which represents success by accepted standards, including the values of successful peers.

Then, they move to an actual *acceptance of failure.* They believe that they're really unable to do or become what's expected of them. By giving up in school, getting kicked out of class, dropping out, or getting thrown out of school, they find confirmation of their beliefs. They actually begin trying to fulfill all the low home and school expectations. A feeling of "I can't win; I will do what I want — to heck with what everyone else thinks" dominates their every move. A belief that "I'll get what I want, regardless of whom I hurt along the way'' becomes their moral condition.

Finally, these students turn to *crime and violence.* It's almost a natural evolution. However, this complete spiral of futility results only if there's no intervention in any one of the various steps. Fortunately, the process can be reversed at any of those points. But there are no jumps in the reversal process. Rather, reversal proceeds upward in the same order that it travels downward. Understanding this reality is vitally important.

Summary

When the various signs of futility appear, we cannot pull away. We must intervene. Our job is to reverse the spiral. However, we must realize that we *cannot skip steps in the reversal process.*

This is the point at which we often make our mistake. When we try to help and don't see a total reversal, we think we've failed. We think the student is neither listening nor learning from us. So we quit. How many times have we said, ''I've talked to him twice and it hasn't done any good,'' or, ''At best, he's only good for a couple of days.'' Likewise, we may recognize a stage and erroneously think a student will outgrow it — so we do nothing.

Sometimes, we also make the mistake of evaluating the situation from our viewpoint, not the students'. Young people tell us how they feel, and we ignore them. Yet, truth for students caught in the spiral is truth as they see it. It's what their minds perceive as truth that counts. If they feel rejected, then they are rejected, whether we think so or not. That's why we must listen to what students tell us — and act accordingly. If we don't, the force of the spiral will certainly keep pulling them downward.

Our job is to help these students back up. Sometimes, insisting on professional help is a must. However, avoiding those first signs of rejection is a big step. Confronting these feelings at this first stage can save both students and us much despair further down the destructive road of futility. Once we recognize which stage the student is in and start the reversal process, we are in a strategic position from which we can resolve the problem — step by step. Unless we take this strategic position, we may quit — sometimes after we have started winning.

The ''Spiral of Futility'' theory was developed by Samuel Proctor of Rutgers University.

PART FIVE

TACT RATHER THAN ATTACK

Strategic Position Rationale: Tact and attack are two strategies which are highly successful, but poles apart. Attack destroys relationships. Tact is the professional strategy which builds the relationship necessary to make behavior change a permanent condition rather than a temporary compliance.

Two things have often been said about human behavior. First is that it's easy to figure out and predict because people want just one thing: their own way. We may laugh at such a statement, but it is true. Second, it's also been said that people, in attempting to get their way, will choose methods that they have learned through experience work for them. That's one of the reasons some people use diplomacy and tact. It's also one of the reasons others choose attack.

Because these two behaviors are at opposite poles, we as professional educators ought to look at both when developing a strategic position in discipline situations. The plain truth is that many people find good and bad in both actions. For instance, some see tact as manipulation and attack as an open and honest stance. Yet, the way people react to the two behaviors may tell us which one is healthy and which is not.

Ways To Motivate

It's widely accepted that there are only two ways to get people to do what we want them to do — and we may find that we use both of these techniques in discipline situations. One way is to make it very *pleasant* for people to do what we want them to do. The other is to make it very *unpleasant* for them *not* to do what we want them to do. Unfortunately, both techniques are highly successful — at least for the short term.

For instance, our routine technique for handling discipline problems may include first trying to be nice, then being harsh if being nice doesn't work. This is a variance in professional approach and foundation — and we need to ask which of the two actions would be best for us to stick to.

Certainly we should realize that to regard tact as manipulation is to regard kindness as deceit. Tact is not manipulation unless that is our specific intent.

But attack is always manipulation — and if we hold the power in a situation, it is manipulation in its crudest form. With tact, however, people can respond through free choice. There is no such choice in response to attack. In truth, tact is empathetic consideration. Attack is a form of forced compliance. The question is: Why do we attack rather than use tact and diplomacy?

A look at the conditions under which we are apt to use attack rather than tact may answer this question. The plain truth is that personal human conditions and circumstances play an important part in our choice of behavior. And this is important for obvious reasons, one of which is that using attack can affect our relations with all people, including students. Remember, our relationship with one student affects our relationships with all students. A look at our classrooms will prove this truth. If we attack a student for asking what we consider a dumb question, for instance, the rest of our students may be thinking, "If you thought that was a dumb question, you should have heard mine." Their attitude then becomes, "I'm not asking any questions in this class."

Conditions Of Choice

Psychologists say we are more prone to use tact when we don't feel a sense of urgency or when we don't fear making a big mistake. Likewise, we are more prone to be tactful when we are rested, calm, and patient. Conversely, we are most likely to attack when we are busy, tired, or hurried. There are two other times when we are most likely to choose attack: when we are defiant, and when we want our own way — immediately. As teachers, we can all benefit from realizing these possibilities.

It would be unrealistic not to admit that many people operate on the premise that the best defense is a good offense. That's why they attack — to keep their weakness hidden or to get their own way. After all, it works. When teachers attack, students capitulate. Yet, a close look will reveal that attack may work only for a short period of time. It pushes students away from us over the long term. That's why attack is not a good professional strategic foundation. Unfortunately, as a defense or a technique to get our own way immediately, we may continue to choose attack over tact. It's a mistake, regardless.

If our fundamental values hold to a recognition that people are important, then we don't want to make it unpleasant for students to do what we want them to do. On the contrary, we want them to do so because we have motivated them to do what we want them to do for healthy and productive reasons. Yet it's a simple reality that conditions can make us choose attack over tact. That's why we need to be aware of these conditions before we act.

Summary

Both tact and attack are behaviors that allow us to motivate students. Both are effective in helping us maintain control and get our own way. Yet, we usually choose attack over tact for very specific reasons.

If we understood the consequences, we would change our course and adopt tact and diplomacy as our strategic position — with the discipline problem as well as with the rest of the class. Attack hurts students. It damages self-concepts. It always degrades, puts students in a subservient position, and negates their opinions, thinking, or contributions. Tact does none of these things. Rather, it holds the best possibility for building. That's why tact is the strategic position we should adopt if we want to change student behavior.

People who lack tact are usually regarded as crude and unrefined. We know that those who attack are always regarded as unprofessional and without dignity. Likewise, they often find themselves in a position in which, although what they say is perfectly right, students react to them as if they were totally wrong. That's the price they pay for attacking.

There are several things we can do to make sure we are tactful. First, we can slow down. We can make sure to listen before we speak, and quiet down first. Most important, we can think of long-term rather than short-term benefits. If we do, we will surely see that how we handle a current situation will affect students in the days ahead. Finally, we can remember to opt for an accepting response rather than forced compliance. This alone will set the tone for what we say and how we say it. Once we discover the benefits of tact for students as well as for ourselves, we will find each successive discipline situation easier to handle and live with. Our students will be grateful for the improvement in our strategic position — and so will we.

PART SIX

YOU CAN'T TAKE IT BACK

Strategic Position Rationale: When handling problems, an adult cannot talk to children differently than he or she would talk to other adults.

There are probably very few of us who at one time or another haven't "put our foot in our mouth" by saying the wrong thing at the wrong time.

How many times have we said something we wish we hadn't? One thing is true for sure: We can't take it back. Oh, how we wish we could.

Sometimes we even think we have been successful in ''smoothing a situation over.'' In truth, we haven't. Only the graciousness of the other person allows us to think that we have. This is to his or her credit, not ours. When it comes to our professional strategic position in discipline situations, we would be wise to remember this truth. That's why we need to ponder the fact that adults may think and act differently when responding to another adult than they do when reacting to a child.

A Difference Which Alters Strategic Position

If there's one thing I have noticed about such ''slips,'' it's that we often think and react differently if that ''slip'' occurs while we're talking to the young. With adults, we are more prone to apologize, or to become quiet very quickly and try to let the embarrassing situation pass. One thing is for sure: With adults we seem to be more aware of what we said and are sorry that we said it. We are also likely to resolve never to make the same mistake again.

That's not always true when we are talking to students. We don't always regard the miscue as being such a serious mistake. We might even rationalize our remarks by thinking or saying to someone else that the student ''deserved it'' or ''had it coming.'' We might even say that our remark needed to be said and add, ''I'm glad I said it.'' We may even laugh about it. But the fact remains that we do often think and react differently toward young people than we do toward adults. Most adults do. This would indicate that adults often respond in a less responsible and sensitive way when they are dealing with the young.

Maybe that's why it's not uncommon for adults to be unaware that they've said something offensive when talking to students. This may be another negative side effect of classifying children as less important than adults. Maybe it's the result of a feeling of superiority that makes one believe, in his or her own way, that adults do not have to account to young people for what they say or do. Regardless, that's one of the reasons adults can hurt young people so much, so quickly, and so easily.

It's one thing to be insulted or mistreated; it's quite another not to be apologized to for the insult or mistreatment. We need to think about these things in our daily relationships with students. They are vitally important in establishing our strategic position in discipline situations.

The Seed Is Planted When We Don't React Professionally

A teacher simply cannot ignore the fact that, once something is said, it's said. And it can't be taken back. An apology is a must, but an apology is made only in the maturity of an aftermath of inconsideration and bad taste. One thing is sure: What you said won't be forgotten. You may forget it, but the student won't.

A teacher has many students, but a student may have but one teacher. A junior high, middle school, or high school student has at most only slightly over half a dozen teachers. That's why students can repeat verbatim what any of their teachers has said to them. Chances are they could repeat these words again six months or a year from the occurrence.

Maybe we aren't aware of some things we say because we deal with so many students in the course of a day. Maybe the fact that we are in touch with so many students has resulted in a kind of carelessness — or even disrespect. Maybe dealing with so many kinds of personalities has caused us to be less sensitive. It shouldn't. It won't if we truly regard and treat each student as an individual regardless of the number of students we teach. A teacher must always think and react professionally, in a human and decent way. Telling a student to "shut up," using the words "dumb" or "stupid," belittling friendships, or "telling a student off" are teacher errors. Too often, words that should never have been spoken are said in countless little incidents. A student blurts out in class, pushes somebody, gets out of line in the cafeteria, runs in the halls, makes noise at assembly, or is rude to another student — and we say something in haste and in anger to resolve the situation quickly. The problem is that what we said and how we said it were not befitting the reaction of a professional teacher. Neither were the remarks worthy of any human being. When such is the case, our strategic position, insofar as changing behavior is concerned, rests on a foundation of sand.

Summary

As teachers, we are responsible for what we say — whenever we say it. A sarcastic remark, a put-down, a public tongue lashing, or a biting comment is always out of order. The fact that these actions have been time-honored, accepted practices for teachers is beside the point. They are neither professional nor characteristic of the strategic positions or practices we want to encourage.

People are people. They react the same regardless of their age. In truth, many of our greatest difficulties arise when we treat people inconsiderately. There are ways to do things — and ways not to do things. We would have many happier students in our schools if we were to speak to and treat students in the way we want to be spoken to and treated ourselves. The problem is that we sometimes don't — especially in regard to discipline problems.

We all make a "slip of the tongue" occasionally. We all say things we shouldn't. When we do, we can't act as if nothing happened. It did. And it happened to a human being. We can do but one thing. It is the same thing we would do with an adult under similar circumstances. We can begin by saying, "I'm sorry" — and mean it. But the real and meaningful healing can begin only when we are strong enough to tell students that our bad manners had to do with us and not with them. Remember, when we err, apology must be a part of our strategic position if we intend to be effective disciplinarians.

PART SEVEN

DON'T BACK YOURSELF AGAINST THE WALL

Strategic Position Rationale: Ultimatums hinder teacher flexibility, close off courses of action, decrease effectiveness in handling misbehavior, and are seldom, if ever, possible to enforce.

Sometimes, teachers actually create the conditions under which discipline problems are incubated. The following are the kinds of teacher statements which generate discipline problems:

- If you fail my final exam, you'll fail this course.
- If you don't like it, that's tough.
- If you do that one more time, you will never be permitted back in this room again.
- Want to see how tough I can be?
- If anyone makes another sound, the whole class will stay after school every night for a week.

Never, never make any of these statements to any of your students under any circumstances. Statements like these give teachers more problems than anything else they do. Such statements take away your strategic position for solving a problem and, without reservation, actually make inappropriate behavior a probability.

No matter what follows these teacher threats, students have heard them before. The fact that they are being used in school instead of at home is merely a shift in time and place. The only difference may be that we, as teachers, carry through our threats to a conclusion while parents don't — or it may be the other way around. The child may expect the punishment to follow the threat at home — but may find that he or she need not bother to listen to teachers, for their threats are always void of action.

Issuing ultimatums is simply a matter of backing yourself against the wall. It's statements like these that put teachers in a position in which they must either carry out a threat or face the problems that result when students find out they don't mean what they say. And many times the threat cannot be carried out.

And if you carry out your threat, you may show unfairness that cannot be tolerated by students, parents, or your colleagues. Even your maturity as an adult or as a professional teacher may be in question. And it is just possible you may overstep the realm of your authority as a classroom teacher. All too often teachers issue ultimatums in desperation and lose their professional strategic position as leaders in the classroom.

Too, remember that whenever you back yourself against the wall as a teacher, the chances are you also back someone else against the wall with you. It is probably your administrator. One of the toughest responsibilities for an administrator is to support a teacher who has used poor judgment or acted beyond the realm of his or her authority — and at the same time do what is in the best interest of students. It is an impossible task. And never get the mistaken idea that just because your administrator "backed you up," you were right. Many times a teacher's decision is enforced by the administrator in the best interest of staff and school morale — even though the administrator knows the teacher's decision was wrong.

A Sign Of Failure

A teacher should examine carefully the use of threats as a motivational tool. More often than not, they make a teacher look weak and foolish. Most teachers are fully aware of this fact. Why, then, do professional teachers use threats? One reason is obvious. Threats are a substitute for effective discipline. When all else fails, threats can become the automatic human response. They are an end result of frustration or of simply not knowing what else to do. That's why threats are weak from the beginning. Most die as soon as they have been uttered and have but one impact: They further deteriorate the teacher's position. That's a fact. Oh yes, a threat may "work" a time or two — until an individual student or the whole class finds out that it is an act of teacher desperation. After that, nothing the teacher does seems to make any real difference.

Sometimes teachers bargain with students by using a threat. They say such things as, "If you don't study, I will give a test," or "If you aren't quiet, we'll have to work five minutes into recess." These are nothing more than "bargaining threats." Never fool yourself into believing this type of bargaining is motivating. It is not. Too, experience will reveal that one threat must usually be followed by another, bigger one.

Perhaps the most idle of all threats is the one in which the student is told that he had better "shape up," or his or her parents will be called. He or she might even be told this two or three times — but the call is never made. Perhaps the worst of all threats is the one we never, even for a moment, intend to carry out. Because of our weariness, anger, or frustration, we boil up inside and issue ultimatums that seem to give us a moment of satisfaction and relief. We threaten suspension and expulsion or promise failure in our course or class. Sometimes, we even threaten a child with the loss of our help as well as our friendship. These are critical threats of consequence to the student, the class, and our relationship with both. They can be overcome only by putting professional intellect and action above spontaneous personal reactions.

All Teacher Action Brings Reaction

With reflection, your experience should reveal that many teachers always seem to be able to figure out what they will do in a given discipline situation "if it ever happens again." The problem is, they don't always consider what the reaction to their action will be. Yet, a law of human behavior tells us that there is a reaction for every action — in a continuing chain. The teacher acts, the student reacts, then the teacher reacts to the student and the process continues. This is a law of human behavior. Therefore, it is always necessary for teachers to attempt to predetermine what the reaction to their action will be — before acting. That is, such prediction is necessary if they want to resolve issues rather than simply cause more problems.

If you always consider possible reactions before you act, you may decide to restructure your initial — as well as subsequent — action. Common sense and a reflection on previous experience will, in most instances, structure your action. Thinking before you act will save you hours of misery and help make you a master of human relationships.

Remember, if you are backed against the wall, you put yourself there. Don't ask someone else to reinforce your lack of judgment or blame someone else for not doing so. And remember, in all your future relationships with students, leave yourself room to operate. Don't put yourself in a strategic position in which your professional status is questioned. Doing so destroys not only your confidence, but also the confidence others have in you.

We all want to do what is best for a student — and the class. We also want to do what will work best for us. Making fair and mature decisions is the responsibility of every educator. One inappropriate action or decision in a school can affect many people. Talk to your administrator about any problems you are having in the classroom. Administrators want to, and must, support their teaching staff — but they must also be allowed to be in a position to give this support without sacrificing school policy or philosophy to save a teacher embarrassment. Before you act, talk to your administrator or a colleague you respect. Then, decide together on professional strategic positions and courses of action. You will be better prepared to handle problem situations.

Summary

Threats are usually ineffective in teaching. They work best for the teacher who uses them least. However, unless they are reasonable and students know they will be carried out, they are of no value at all — and most threats can't be carried out. Therefore, threats only put the teacher in a position of disadvantage.

A threat must never violate privacy. If a child is humiliated in the presence of classmates with an angry threat from an angry teacher — even if the threat is carried out — that student won't easily forgive the misuse of teacher authority and power. It is very hard indeed, at times, not to make a threat openly to a child. Yet, it is an absolute must for a teacher never to make this mistake. If the reason for this is not quite clear, try to remember a time when you were on the receiving end of humiliation. Nothing can justify teacher vengeance. Compassion must always be our companion. When it is not, our actions can be worse than the wrong we are punishing. A professional educator must remember there is a consequence of significance within every teacher technique. The consequence contained in a threat is seldom good for a teacher or students.

Backing oneself against the wall is the kind of mistake that might be expected from a new and inexperienced teacher, but not from a mature professional. Threats and ultimatums are usually made in haste and anger, and seldom with thought and intelligence. As teachers, we know threats are not effective. Yet, some teachers will issue an ultimatum at every crisis — and find themselves "between a rock and a hard place" as a result of their action on almost every occasion.

Observe your fellow teachers. You'll never find Master Teachers between a rock and a hard place — with students, parents, faculty, or administrators.

They use their sixth sense, common sense, and it tells them threats and ultimatums usually bring negative reactions from all human beings. They also know all actions bring reactions, and, before making decisions that affect others, they consult with those involved. They realize threats influence both present and future relationships with students, and would never do anything to jeopardize their strategic position as professional teachers.

PART EIGHT

DUE PROCESS: A REQUIREMENT FOR FAIRNESS

Strategic Position Rationale: Fairness is a teacher responsibility which can become a reality in the classroom only when a teacher adopts a plan of due process. It is due process which allows us to deal with each student and situation individually — and this is what fairness is all about.

"Fair" is a big word to young people. In fact, it may be the biggest and most important word of all to students. Certainly, there are few who have ever stepped before a class who have not, at one time or another, had their fairness challenged in a discipline problem situation. If such a challenge hasn't been made to their faces, they can be assured their fairness has been questioned behind their backs. And there are few of us who really don't try to be fair with students regardless of their ability or behavior.

The questions are: What is fair? And who should determine what's fair and what isn't? Equally important to teachers, who are responsible for what goes on in the classroom, is the question: Is it possible or feasible to employ fairness in all discipline cases?

In Almost Every Discipline Situation, Kids Can Question Our Fairness

These are vitally important questions to every teacher. That's because unless a teacher is seen as fair in the eyes of students, he or she may never be trusted or respected. Without being regarded as fair, a teacher may not be able to relate to kids. Likewise, without positive relations, it's difficult to motivate students and form the student-teacher partnership necessary to change misbehavior.

If we asked students, we might be surprised at how often this characteristic called fairness gets in the way of teacher effectiveness and prevents teachers from finding success. That's why it's a subject that needs discussing. Yet, the scope of activities which requires teacher fairness is so broad that it can be overwhelming. After all, fairness is not an issue in only one area of the teacher-student relationship. It includes more than handling discipline problems. There's rule fairness. Then, there are fair tests, fair assignments, fair evaluations, and fair treatment. Too, one can't forget fair grades and requirements. The list is endless. In almost every aspect of school life, students can question our fairness. Herein lies the problem, and the need for our adopting a professional strategic position of fairness.

There is also much we can teach students about fairness. We must teach such lessons. Unfortunately, we may find it difficult to apply our teaching to the day-to-day life in the classroom. And this contradiction can get us in trouble. When it does, we may try to make broad general rules about fairness. This is our first strategic mistake. Life is too comprehensive in a classroom to permit us to make a blanket rule about fairness. Such a broad-based generalization may, in fact, be fair or unfair. Unfortunately, however, it's not feasible.

Fairness Lies In Our Structure Which Allows The Ways And The Means To...

The biggest reason blanket rules regarding fairness don't work is that what's fair for one student may not be fair for another. Nothing is so unfair as the equal treatment of unequals. The ''A'' student is not the same as the one who is failing. Nor are kids who work hard and obey the rules the same as those who couldn't care less.

The problem is that we must be fair. The question is: How can we be fair? The answer lies in our structure. In simple terms, it lies in our procedure for due process. Here, equal procedure rather than equal treatment is our goal — and our strategic position.

First, we must have a standard which is flexible, but all-inclusive. Second, we must talk to students about their responsibilities. We can say, ''It is your responsibility as a member of this group to obey and abide by all the rules of the classroom. However, it is *also your responsibility* as a member of this class to try to change unfair rules.''

Third, our responsibility is to set up a simple due process procedure through which grievances can be heard and rules changed. The procedure must work, both for us and for the students in our classrooms. It must give students a viable procedure for being heard and for changing the rules. If we want to guarantee fairness, our system of due process should also contain procedures which allow students to go to others in authority if they so desire.

Like it or not, these requirements are necessary if we want to be fair — and be regarded as fair. With a structure which contains such allowances, none can claim that our classroom procedures aren't fair. On the contrary, the procedural foundation for fairness is firm.

We must be regarded as fair by those we teach. Yet, we don't always have the time to spend deciding what's fair in every discipline situation encountered in the classroom. It's just not feasible to do so. And it's this reality that may cause us to set up a structure which prevents fairness.

We can, however, spend time with students, mutually accepting the steps available for due process. And we can spend considerable time teaching the rights, privileges, and responsibilities of due process. Too, we can devote time to following up each case, making sure the right lessons were learned. Adopting a strategic position of due process needs our consideration. That's because it can assure our success.

Summary

Due process makes fairness a reality in the classroom and the school. It makes fairness a positive. And due process allows us to treat each student and situation individually. This, in truth, is what fairness is — and what students as well as teachers really want in handling misbehavior.

Be aware that what each young person wants is to be treated as a person — and not to be defined in terms of rules. Due process is the procedure which allows us to treat each student as a person. This is, indeed, fairness at its best and gives us the best chance to correct misbehavior and make the change permanent. Therefore, a teacher must adopt a strategic position which includes due process if he or she is to attain a reputation for fairness.

PART NINE

ABSOLUTELY REFUSE TO REJECT

Strategic Position Rationale: A teacher does not have the prerogative to reject a student, because inclusion rather than exclusion is necessary if a teacher intends to remain positioned to lead and teach.

Nearly all of us have been guilty of rejecting students from time to time for misbehavior. Though there are times when we purposely reject, most of the time we don't willingly choose rejection. Yet, reflection will reveal that we usually reject at a time when our position as teachers is challenged in one form or another. Maybe a child openly opposed or defied us. Sometimes we reject kids when they don't measure up to, or fail to meet, our standards. On the other hand, sometimes our rejection is the result of prejudice. We simply reject because we don't like the way a student looks, dresses, or maintains his or her personal appearance. That's our humanness revealed.

We often disguise our reasons for rejecting students. When our patience ends abruptly or we don't have the answer to a request or question, we may dismiss a child curtly. Make no mistake, this is rejection. Likewise, we may direct a cruel joke at the stubborn or headstrong student. When we choose to put a youngster down in any way, we have chosen rejection. Never think for a moment that we haven't.

We need to be aware that when adults use rejection against children, it is usually a power play. Adults know *before they use power* that the child is powerless to respond. Unfortunately, the cut inherent in rejection usually brings down everything in its path. To bring down those who are already defenseless does not qualify as a heroic act. As teachers, we need to be aware of this classroom reality. If we have a sense of shame after such a rejection, at least we have a point from which to begin. Let us hope that our sense of caring is such that we want to begin making sure we are never guilty of rejecting a child for any reason. We may reject what kids do. But we should never reject them as human beings. This is our guidepost with regard to rejection when working with students who are misbehaving.

A Bad Choice

We can begin developing a professional strategic position by knowing that when we choose to reject a child on a personal basis, we have made a wrong choice. Next, we can ask why we had to go in this direction. A good many of us might have to say that it seemed the easiest thing to do at the time. There are always those children who trigger our unfortunate need for occasional vengeance. Children who are openly aggressive or who are constant class problems are two examples. Their opposites are the vulnerable youngsters whose meek demeanors almost invite mistreatment. Often, rejection in some form is the most available weapon at hand. Our mistake is in thinking that we need any weapon at all.

Sometimes, when we sense that control is drifting away from us, we *think* we can reestablish order and control by a quick act of rejection. We can't. We only hurt a student deeply, and effect a widening disconnection between us and the entire class in the process.

We also need to recognize that we may reject because of our anger, our own insecurity, or our own low self-esteem. If we can come to understand this possibility, we can deal with our urges to reject. When we are no longer afraid of being put down ourselves, we will have no need to offer rejection to any other person. This happens as we gain self-acceptance — and not before. That's a fact. As teachers, we have an obligation to see that we never reject our students. But our commitment goes even deeper. We also need to teach children about rejection.

Summary

We do not have the right — morally or professionally — to reject students personally. Our responsibility is to make adjustments by using our skills, rather than to make exclusions by using power. Also, we need to realize that we help improve the mental health of our students if we can talk with them about the incidents of rejection that do occur. If we can be open and honest with our students, we can replace despairing attack with caring confrontation. There is a difference. Next time you want to reject, pull that student toward you. Talk to the student. Tell him or her of your concern as well as your frustrations. Ask what you can do together. Try to make an agreement in partnership rather than an act of dissolution and you will establish the strategic position necessary to change behavior.

Rejection is a death blow to student and teacher alike. It is final. It separates us from the student-teacher union necessary for the resolution of anything. Worse, it may cause other students to pull away from us too.

If we are convinced that rejection is always negative, we can refuse to use it. It's as simple as that. We don't have to use it — we only think we do. If we are really caring people who are in teaching because we want to help children learn, we will gladly pull away from using a destructive force. And if we have a bad day and find ourselves tempted to use this unprofessional kind of power, we can still avoid succumbing to the temptation by remembering the price of repair. In view of the fact that not one single good thing can be said for using rejection, let's ask ourselves why we ever thought we needed to use it in the first place. Then, let us make inclusion rather than exclusion a part of our strategic position in handling discipline problems.

PART TEN

NO SARCASM

Strategic Position Rationale: Because sarcasm is both unprofessional and always punitive beyond its intentions, it has no place in the classroom.

There are several kinds of human actions that need, I think, to be looked at closely. One such action is sarcasm. It is a communication offering and response that always seems to be at our fingertips — and that always seems to get us into trouble. Yet, for one reason or another, we often persist in utilizing it over and over again in some of our relationships with students. We know before we use sarcasm that we shouldn't, and our feelings confirm the fact after we use it — but we do it again and again in spite of our intellect which tells us we shouldn't. Therefore, to develop a professional strategic position for encouraging appropriate behavior, sarcasm must be eliminated from our actions.

There's One Person Sarcasm Never Passes By...The Victim

There are many kinds of sarcasm which take several different forms, but they all produce the same results. Certainly, they all appear the same to the receiver. It is only from the user's point of view that they differ.

For instance, there is the subtle use of sarcasm. That's the kind we use when we "sneak in" a snide remark or comment that we pretend should go past unnoticed. It's easy to do. We can whisper a belittling comment to another while a student is talking, or we can raise our eyebrows and shake our heads to other students when a child repeatedly fails to turn in homework or when a student answers a question incorrectly. But subtle sarcasm never passes by one person — the victim.

Then there is the blunt and open use of sarcasm. It's used when we want a certain student as well as everyone else to hear what we say. And they do. We can tell a student to "use your head instead of your mouth," or say, "What did I ever do to deserve getting you in class?"

Yet, both the subtle and the blunt sarcastic approaches have the same effect. Somebody is hurt. Everybody feels worse after either approach has been used. Assuredly, no one forgives — nor will anyone be likely to forget quickly. No matter what we call it, sarcasm is a strategic mistake. It is a terrible way to treat people — and we all know it. Professionally, it is inexcusable.

Yet people continue to use it. But why?

"Why" is difficult to answer — but "when" it is most likely to be used does not offer so much mystery. Perhaps a closer look at the times when a teacher is more apt to succumb to its use may offer some caution signals that can prove helpful.

Signals Of Caution

Sarcasm is probably most often used when we are dealing with students we have trouble liking. It is such an easy "put-down," especially if we believe the student to be acting or feeling superior to us or what we are doing. We need only remember that when we attempt to "cut students down to size," we never do. But we do prove what size we are, and it is always smaller than the person to whom we are sarcastic.

Fatigue can also bring out the sarcastic side of one's personality. When a teacher is tired, a quick, snide remark such as, "How much help do you need?" or "If you would spend as much time studying as you do fooling around ..." will get rid of the most persistent student. It will free a teacher of student responsibilities quickly. The same is true when we are mad, upset, or when we are obviously in the wrong. Sarcasm can seem to get us off the hook quickly. It shows others that we don't want to be bothered or that we are really disinterested — and they will leave us alone quickly.

That's one of the big problems with sarcasm. As an escape, it works. It rids a teacher of responsibility and people. In addition, there may be a momentary degree of enjoyment in expelling sarcasm. A teacher might be a little sorry for what he or she said, but may add, "She had it coming, and I'm glad I said it." One may even reason that, "I've wanted to say that for a long time and I feel better as a result of having said it."

That's the way it often is for people who use sarcasm as a human relations approach. They get a certain amount of satisfaction and pleasure from its use. In addition, it offers them an effective defense because others shy away from sarcastic people. Also, it gives them a very formidable offensive weapon. And that is exactly what sarcasm is — a weapon. It is a human relations weapon that bites, stings, hurts, and produces bitterness, and its effects are lasting as well as deadly. The question is: Who is really hurt the most by its use — the giver or the receiver?

Summary

Somehow, sarcasm seems to give its users a false sense of power and intellect. This is one of the things that makes it so very deceiving — and probably the reason some use it as a strategic position in discipline situations more than they should. It produces a mistaken feeling of cleverness, comedy, and superiority in its users. Many people confuse sarcasm with wit. However, these emotions are only shams which deceive the wielder of sarcasm.

Sarcasm is always punitive beyond its intentions, and this should be the clue that proves to its users that their self-image of cleverness and wit is false. Teachers can never forget that sarcasm has no place in the classroom. They must remember that sarcasm is always personal — too personal. And that's what makes it hurt so much. *Generally, it does contain a measure of objective truth.* That's why it is so damaging to students. Everyone recognizes that portion of truth in its contents. This — coupled with the fact that it is usually offered by someone close to the victim — close enough to know his or her faults anyway — makes sarcasm a weapon which discharges unmatched pain.

Sarcasm makes a lasting impression that neither the mind nor the heart can forget. It tears relationships between humans to the point at which separation is sought. That's why sarcasm is the alienator that must be alien to teachers as a strategic position if they intend to guide children in a human and caring way.

PART ELEVEN

CARING IS NOT CODDLING

Strategic Position Rationale: Coddling supports weakness. Caring develops strengths. Without caring, all teacher methods and techniques lose their weight and may be regarded by students as manipulation.

There are some words which can stiffen a teacher's spine the moment they are mentioned. *Coddling* is such a word. We know exactly how we feel about adults who advocate coddling children. If those adults are teachers, we're really turned off. Coddling children is pampering them. There's absolutely no place in the school or classroom for either as far as we are concerned. The word has such bad connotations that we may find it hardly a discussible issue. Yet, when we talk about caring, words like coddling can pop into our minds. But caring is not coddling. And we should never think for a moment that it is.

While Coddling Is Totally Negative, Caring Has An Entirely Different Weight And Intention

Like-sounding words such as caring and coddling can cloud our reasoning. Yet, there's a big difference between the two definitions. As professional educators, we need to understand this vast difference if we want to be effective in our work with young people.

None of us can quarrel with the negative aspects of coddling students. When we pamper children, we only support their weaknesses. If we help students to be excused for no good reason, we don't offer healthy standards for them to measure themselves against. Helping students establish bad reasons for not performing well is not our task — and can only be crippling. Therefore, it's safe to say that coddling students is something we don't want to do in our classrooms or in the school.

A close look will reveal that caring is really the exact opposite of coddling. While coddling is totally negative, caring is positive. Caring has an entirely different intention. Above all, caring has benefits for teachers and students alike that cannot be overlooked if a teacher wants to be successful in handling all students, including discipline problems. That's why we need to know that caring is the foundation of our professional strategic position, the focal point of our teaching style, and the tone of the climate in our classrooms.

Caring Requires Structure — And Something Else That We May Fear Giving Students

One reason it can be said that caring is the opposite of coddling is that caring requires structure. The best example I can offer of the structure required in caring is to share with you the conversation I overheard between three girls at a school party.

The first girl told her friends, "I have to be in by 11:30 p.m." The second girl said, "My parents said I had to be home by midnight." The third girl said, "I can stay out as late as I wish — my parents don't care what time I come home."

Like caring parents, the teacher who cares about young people provides structure — and for the same obvious reasons. However, another requirement of caring may not be so obvious — and may be one of the reasons some teachers are afraid to care.

That's because caring requires an investment in students. It requires involvement. Coddling does not. Caring also requires giving. Coddling may only mean giving in.

Caring requires kindness. And kindness is not weakness. But coddling reveals an adult weakness which can be misleading and destructive to young people. As professionals, we need to recognize that without caring, all teacher techniques can be seen by students as manipulation, especially in discipline situations. That's why a teacher can't develop with students the relationships necessary for learning without making caring a part of his or her professional strategic position.

Summary

We must hold the welfare of each student as our fundamental value in everything we do in disciplining students. Teacher caring is the professional foundation which allows us to hold to this value during our ups and downs, good days and bad. Caring is our personal and professional stabilizer, especially in handling kids who misbehave.

Caring gives us sensitivity. It helps us listen to kids. It keeps us approachable. Caring motivates us to take risks and stands — especially regarding value positions. Caring lets us allow failure. Caring does not mean giving kids unlimited options or choices. Neither does it mean that we should or must give advice on every occasion. After all, children must learn to make decisions. Caring is, however, the vehicle which allows us to reach our potential in teaching. Without caring as a strategic position, a teacher simply can't do the job.

Caring must be revealed in everything we do. It's demonstrated in the way we give tests, the assignments we give, the way we correct misbehavior, and the promptness with which we grade and return papers. Our caring comes through loud and clear to students. Our lack of caring comes through loud and clear as well.

Caring is one of our finest motivational tools in discipline situations. That's because it's an investment in students as well as an involvement in what we're trying to do for them. Certainly, no student can ask for more than to have a teacher who cares. After all, caring support from concerned adults is one of the strengths students need in order to find a satisfying and meaningful life, now as well as in the future. That's why every teacher needs to adopt caring as a professional strategic position to be effective in managing appropriate as well as inappropriate student behavior. And a close look will reveal that, too often, our big discipline problems begin when we start giving in and stop being involved in changing behavior.

PART TWELVE

REMEMBER, YOU MAY BE STARTING THE FIGHT

Strategic Position Rationale: Teacher respect for the student is a vital element in problem situations, regardless of the respect being offered by the student — and loss of power is often the cause of disrespect on both sides of the desk.

Disciplining a student in the presence of a class requires special techniques. That is, it does it you want to change a behavior rather than start a fight. Behaviorists say aggression emerges from feelings of powerlessness when one is confronted publicly. This may explain why both a teacher's and a student's temper can flare instantly in discipline situations. Loss of power may lie at the root of the problem. Here are some suggestions which facilitate correcting behavior rather than beginning a struggle in discipline situations.

Three Responses Are Likely

Remember, respect is needed *more* in problem situations than in normal ones. If we tell students to "shut up," "keep quiet," or "do it or else," one of three responses is likely. First, they can blurt back a similar disrespectful comment. Second, they can say nothing, wait until we are out of earshot, and then "bad mouth" us to every classmate who will listen. Third, they can sit quietly without emotion — and think it's okay for someone to talk to them in such a manner. Unfortunately, we lose with any of these responses. In addition, we may expect the third response and think all is well when we get it — or be angered if we get the first response and hurt if someone tells us about a student talking about us behind our backs.

Remember, even when students misbehave, only by responding in respectful ways do we hold our professional strategic position as teachers, and teach the lessons we want students to learn. And remember, when we correct one student, the rest of the class is witness to, and influenced by, our handling of the situation.

To maintain a respectful strategic position when disciplining, we should ask ourselves three questions and make the answers a part of our *conditioned action responses*. First, "Do I always have to win?" Second, "What normal responses can I expect from my actions?" Third, "How can I lighten the situation rather than make it more stressful?'' These may seem like simple questions. They are not. And our answers may determine our success in handling misbehavior because our *strategic position* affects the *strategic action* we will take. This is why this subject is presented in the last section of strategic position — and preceding the first section regarding strategic action.

We simply can't think in terms of winning and losing in discipline situations. Neither should the misbehavior of students bring forth equally bad behavior by the teacher. Once we adopt this professional strategic position, then we can also decide which battles should be fought and when — and feel comfortable with, rather than diminished or frustrated by, our decisions. That's because simply deciding has allowed us to keep control and power.

Common sense should tell us that kids need to feel important too — and that this need will necessitate concessions, draws, and ''back-offs'' by both students and teachers. Perspective should indicate to us that the classroom should be a place where both teacher and students feel significant. If our discipline plan contains only the means to render kids powerless, we have set the stage for aggression — on their part and on ours. And our choice has put us in the strategic position of initiating the fight.

Power is a secondary human need. This need is within us all. We need to understand it. Because of our fear of losing power in discipline situations, we may actually be responsible for creating damaging and defeating confrontations with kids. Likewise, because of our unwillingness to share power with students, we may be motivated into confrontations which could be avoided. That's why we must remember that the secondary need for power is present in children as well as adults. How we handle our power as teachers can start or stop negative and unproductive confrontations.

As We Discipline, A Class Monitors Our Actions

With this in mind, we should remember not to constantly raise our voices, or belittle or threaten a student we are disciplining. We should also remember never to touch students or grab articles from them when they're mad. If a student pokes a classmate with a pencil, for instance, don't grab the pencil. And never grab and break it. Remember, other students — and maybe the entire class — are monitoring our actions. What we do may make or break our relations with all kids. Never forget, how *well* or *badly* we act may make it *hard* or *easy* to teach future lessons about appropriate behavior to all students. And it may render meaningless our words regarding help, caring, respect, consideration, and cooperation.

I remember an elementary student who was using earphones without permission. The teacher told her to put them down. She didn't. Finally, the teacher pulled the earphones from her head. The child cried; the teacher let her cry, and said the child "deserved" a little pain. Later, two students got into a fight and one got hurt. The teacher stopped class to talk about how important it was not to hurt people. When she finished, the little girl raised her hand and said, "But you hurt me this morning and said it was okay."

No matter how mad we get, we must be careful about what we say and how we react. If we aren't careful, we may not be teaching that respect is a two-way street. When we say, "Do it or else," the stage is set for confrontation. And power is the problem on both sides of the desk. That's why this issue of winning and losing needs our professional consideration. Our decision will affect our professional strategic position — and subsequent action — in every discipline situation. Too often, unfortunately, it's the teacher who causes the fight. Worse, because of an inappropriate strategic position, the teacher may do and say things that often turn out to be worse than the behavior he or she is correcting.

Summary

Saying such things as, "Give it to me or I'll take it from you," sets the stage for negative reactions. When things go wrong, a teacher must be an adjustor — not a dictator. Here is where we use our skill to solve rather than perpetuate a difficulty.

Fighting fire with fire seldom works, even though we can all give examples in which it did. However, the opposite approach often does work. That's why respect is such a valuable teaching tool. It must be a part of your strategic position. Respect requires decency, not demands. It encourages both listening and talking in considerate ways. It offers the foundation for healing rather than hurting. Above all, once an incident has passed, respect helps us maintain the relationship necessary for teaching. And this consideration must be included in your strategic position.

Certainly, we seldom intend to start a fight in the classroom. Yet, once a struggle begins, we're automatically involved because of our position as classroom teachers. If we must have the last word, or if we have a distorted professional perspective regarding this thing called winning and losing, we may win every battle and lose every war. If we know that there doesn't have to be either a winner or a loser, we will approach every discipline problem knowing that the teacher, the student, and other members of the class can benefit from the outcome.

CHAPTER 4

STRATEGIC ACTION

PART ONE

YOUR FIRST STRATEGIC ACTION DECISION

Before you can even begin resolving a discipline problem, you must make a professional strategic action decision. *You must ask yourself what you want.* Do you want to punish a student or change a behavior? This is a very important question. And you must decide where your primary emphasis lies.

If punishment is a must, then so be it. Just know that when punishment is your primary consideration and action, all other professional ideas or suggestions for handling misbehavior may be unsatisfactory in your eyes.

Before you adopt a *punishment only* stance, however, you might ask yourself a question. Have you ever, in any way, been a problem or acted in inappropriate ways? If you're among those few who have never acted inappropriately in any way, it may be hard for you to understand why students do. Likewise, it may be difficult for you to think in terms other than swift, hard, and consistent punishment. Also, you may spend time and effort dealing in rules and regulations and the punishments for violating them. Yet, if you want students to become self-disciplined, you must devote time to discovering the reasons for misbehavior, the needs students are revealing via behavior, and appropriate ways to meet those needs so that children will behave appropriately. For instance, many students misbehave in order to be successful. Wrong as it is, they're trying to avoid failure in the only way they see possible. Unless we can help them find success in appropriate ways, they will probably continue misbehaving.

Tiny Consequences...Fast Chances

Too often, however, we think in terms of punishment and reprimand to teach a lesson — and that's fine. Yes, it is fine. The mistake lies not in punishment or reprimand — but in the *big* punishment and the *big* reprimand.

If you want to teach students to admit their mistakes, learn from them, *and go on* — you must adopt two strategic actions. First, think in terms of *tiny* consequences. Second, give students *fast* chances to repair their situation. The tiny consequence is self-explanatory. Just don't make a big deal out of every misbehavior.

The fast chance is easy to interpret too. It means giving students a quick way to mend a fence or correct a situation. Too often, we do just the opposite. Yet, we know that people don't function well when they are in trouble with the boss. Students aren't the exception. Until things are made right, they may not do well insofar as classroom studies are concerned.

Third, give students options, or ways to get out of trouble. Don't let students struggle alone with difficulty. Rather, help them seek solutions. Inclusion rather than exclusion must be our stance. Therefore, if we want to resolve discipline problems, we must first decide *what we want* and *what stance we intend to take*. If swift and severe punishment is our primary consideration, it is unlikely that tiny consequences, fast chances to repair, and giving options will be our strategic actions. And if we intend to teach a class and have kids focus attention on their studies, they must be.

PART TWO

THE PRIVATE CONFERENCE

Strategic Action Rationale: Handling discipline problems publicly is the greatest form of disrespect a teacher can reveal to students and often results in the greatest amount of disrespect students give to teachers.

The private teacher-student conference is a must for dealing with the wide range of conflicts and misbehaviors that occur within a classroom. It is one of the most effective, yet least used, of all teacher tools and actions. We say we don't have time for such conferences. In reality, we don't have time not to have them if we want to teach — and not spend our time handling the same misbehavior in the same students every day of the year. Every teacher would be wise to begin developing and polishing his or her private teacher-student conference technique, because such procedure must be a part of the successful teacher's professional strategic position. Without it, very few students who are misbehaving will be managed effectively, because acceptable behavior will not be learned via public confrontation.

Built-In Benefits Of One-On-One Management

Private counsel rather than public correction has unmatched natural benefits for teacher and student alike. The private conference gives a teacher a greater probability for success in solving both behavioral and academic problems. The one-on-one strategy almost always does. It builds a relationship between two people because it is personal and private. Too, it does not put students in a position where they feel they are being "watched" by their peers. The need to respond, to save face, or to seek attention that intensifies many teacher-student confrontations is greatly reduced and may be eliminated. Privacy is vital in correcting and changing student behavior as well as in teaching acceptable behavior.

One of the biggest advantages of the private conference is found in the fact that when this strategic position is adopted, counseling always comes later — not at the time of an infraction. This is good for the student and the class, as well as the teacher. It gives everyone time to cool off, think objectively, and react in ways that will improve the situation. Too, it gives the teacher an extra advantage. One of the first rules a teacher should learn about teacher-student conflict is to neutralize the circumstances and the environment. The weighted environment of a classroom filled with other students, and a charged circumstance, put a teacher at a disadvantage. A quiet, empty classroom offers both teacher and student a better chance for success because it facilitates results rather than reactions. So does the time delay. Remember, time can work for and against you in changing behavior. Certain steps must be taken immediately. Other steps must be taken later, in follow-up, counseling, and teaching.

When two people sit down privately and focus complete attention on the problem at hand, without other distractions, positive results are more likely to occur. There aren't thirty other young people waiting for a lesson. There are no lessons to teach, bells to ring, nor emotional feelings hanging heavy, ready to burst in the air. There are no other students purposely trying to interfere with a solution. There are just a teacher and a student with a problem to solve.

Individualized, personalized, and sincere teacher assistance is then a reality, and the teacher has a chance to be effective. An administrator can't solve individual teacher problems in the presence of the entire staff in a faculty meeting. Neither can teachers solve all their individual student behavior and academic problems in full view of the entire class. Yet, in too many instances, this is exactly what we try to do.

Your Strategic Approach Is Vital

One can never forget that the responsibility for the tone of the private conference rests solely with the teacher. The student is not the professional. The teacher is. The student is the variable, while the teacher is the constant. Regardless of student behavior or actions during the conference, the teacher must establish and maintain a helpful, caring, competent, and professional atmosphere. A child can be ready to quit. This is his or her prerogative. A teacher has many prerogatives too, but quitting is not one of them. When we are helpless, we must seek help. Referral is our prerogative. Even here, however, we must remain level-headed, and take recommendations, but not quit.

To establish the correct atmosphere for a conference, approach in the beginning is of vital importance. Though the core of the conference cannot be discussed in this writing because each is of a different nature, we can talk about the general guidelines for beginning all conferences.

First, always remember that this is a meeting between two human beings. Never forget that there are always two sides, and listening, without interruption, is one reason you made arrangements for a private conference. We will discuss this subject in the next chapter. Remember, however, that in this private situation kids should have greater latitude for expressing their opinions without being regarded as disrespectful. Too, the meeting was not arranged to present a teacher with an opportunity for attack. Few behavior problems are solved with battles. The purpose of the private conference should not be to humiliate, or to point out each and every weakness in the student's character either. The objective is to bring student and teacher closer together, not to tear them further apart.

This situation, then, is an opportunity for two-way communication that you, as a professional teacher, have arranged to help one of your students. Never lose sight of this fact or let the student think otherwise. This stance must be a known fact regarding your professional strategic position. It must be unalterable.

Therefore, gentleness rather than harshness, questioning rather than giving answers, and acceptance rather than rejection must be the climate. In any human relationship, you may disapprove of what a person does, but you cannot disapprove of the person. As I have said previously, when a teacher mistakenly rejects a student rather than his or her behavior, all is lost. This fact must never be misunderstood or violated, or the gap between teacher and student will widen to irreparable proportions. Then, changing inappropriate student behavior is less likely — except changes which are gained temporarily through raw power. And it is unwise to turn your back on a student who has been forced to capitulate to such power. Likewise, don't expect this student to be supportive of you where other students are concerned. Rather, look for the student to use his or her power with peers to bring your house down at every opportunity.

The beginning of the private conference is the time when many teachers fail. Though their hearts may be in the right place, all is destroyed in the first minutes of the conference. Not getting the expected student response, they say too much.

The first few seconds of the teacher-student conferences have much to do with the success or failure of the meeting. It is then, more than at any other time, that the teacher lays the groundwork for a successful conference. Teacher appearance, preparation, approach, and projected attitude toward a student in a conference are vital. The importance of the teacher's first words cannot be minimized. Contrary to belief, student attitude is of little importance in the beginning of the conference. It is teacher attitude that can turn discipline problems around.

A teacher's first words, in effect, govern the conference climate as well as the student's behavior and receptiveness. Teachers would be wise to give their first words careful thought. Certainly, the first sentence must not be a reprimand. Here are some tips regarding your beginning words. The next time you have a conference, begin by saying: "I asked you to meet with me today because I was wondering if: ... there was something I could do for you regarding the difficulty we had in class today. ... you thought the work in class was too hard. ... you were having trouble doing your homework. ... someone or something was bothering you in class today. ... we could discuss your behavior before it becomes a serious problem."

These first words are all-important. Their tone, inflection, and sincerity can turn a discipline problem around. All these strategic approaches are disarming for a number of reasons. They are not accusatory. They do not demand or judge. Rather, they grant the student both authority and responsibility. Equally important, they are solution-seeking. And they are unexpected — that's the biggest reason they are disarming. Even if the student launches into a complaint, you are positioned to help and seek opinions regarding a solution. Then, the student is *part of the solution.* Never forget — until a student buys into the problem, he or she will not buy into the solution of that problem. And this is a primary requisite for changing behavior.

Teachers have long complained that it is difficult to find time to meet with students on an individual basis. However, there are many times and places that a meeting between teacher and student can take place. Before and after school have traditionally been the best times. However, private meetings can also take place between classes, during recess and lunch periods, and even in the back of the room during study time, as long as nobody else is aware of the nature of the discussion.

Special arrangements can even be made with other teachers to utilize conference periods for these vitally important meetings. In talking with colleagues, you may find they are having similar difficulties with a particular student. They may welcome your meeting with this student during a class of theirs which coincides with your conference period. Of course, this is a joint decision of both teachers. However, there is just one rule: Discuss your situation only, and never speak of the other teacher or class to the student under any circumstances or for any reason.

When you offer your help without condemnation, the stage is set for a meaningful private conference. You have upgraded yourself without degrading the student. Even hostile feelings toward you as a teacher can now be discussed. You have seen to this possibility. Now, you can both make promises to each other, and you both have established a strategic position to change unacceptable behavior into acceptable behavior. It's strange, but you will probably be able to talk about *anything* and both come away feeling better about yourselves and each other.

Summary

Too many teachers "throw in the towel" regarding students, thinking they have done everything when, indeed, they have done nothing. In truth, they have said too many of the wrong things. They and their students have talked too much in public and not enough in private.

A "recap" of teacher action with children who misbehave often shows that students have been sent to the office or the counselor, given demerits, deprived of privileges, and reprimanded in the classroom many, many times. Yet, teachers can often count on one hand the times they have had a private and in-depth conference with these students. When this is the case, the strategic position which offers the most workable approach has been ignored. The one-on-one situation, with its built-in teacher advantages, has been overlooked or used only on a minimal basis.

One need not worry about the outcome of the private teacher-student conference. There are few teachers who cannot set into motion solutions for the majority of their classroom problems — if they begin handling them on a one-on-one basis, and if they remember always to approach them from a professional rather than a personal viewpoint.

PART THREE

GET BOTH VIEWPOINTS

Strategic Action Rationale: It's a waste of teacher time and effort to proceed in problem solving before finding out what the issues are in the eyes of students, and sharing with students the teacher's perspective.

If asked, we could list the names of students along with the specific nature of each of their behavior problems. That's why it might surprise us to know that what we believe to be the cause of the misbehavior may not be the problem at all. At least it may not be the real problem as far as the student is concerned. If we think differently, we're probably mistaken. That's because there are always two vital viewpoints in every discipline problem — the teacher's and the student's. And it's amazing how often they differ. We could solve many more discipline problems if we would take one strategic action before beginning — get both viewpoints. Therefore, getting both viewpoints, yours and the student's, must be your *first* action. The teacher who proceeds without this input may be trying to go upstream without a paddle. This is another argument for the private conference in resolving discipline problems.

Definite Steps

With every discipline problem, try these professional strategic action steps. They may save you hours of time and frustration searching for possible solutions. They may also help you find solutions with amazing ease and quickness.

First, as discussed in the previous section, arrange a private conference. Again, make sure it's a friendly one rather than one you call because of anger or hostility. Your purpose for the conference is twofold: You want to give and to get information. Therefore, tell the student the purpose of the meeting. Use the beginning approach discussed in the previous section. Listen to the student's response, then relate in simple and direct terms what you see and what you believe the problem to be. For instance, you may say,

''This is how I perceive the problem. You are always talking and pestering classmates, and you don't listen to what is being said in class.'' After you have stated your opinion, simply say, ''This is how I see the problem. Now, how do you see it?'' Don't let your question receive a shallow answer. Dig to find out what the student is *thinking and feeling — and why*. Don't end the meeting until you know every detail, big or small.

This is a vitally important procedure for two reasons. First, if the student does not see the problem as you do, he or she will not accept responsibility for the problem. Second, without such acceptance, a student will not participate in the solution. That's why you must have mutual agreement on the whole problem. If a student won't tell you, you must use the support of a counselor and principal to help you find out.

More often than not, you'll find that the student's opinion differs somewhat or totally from yours. Equally important, you'll be surprised at how often the problem is being caused by something small, insignificant, or even unrelated. For instance, you might see a student's behavior as a clear case of dislike and disrespect, while the student claims the misbehaving is caused by your treating others better than you do him or her. Or you might see the problem as being caused by the student not paying attention in class, while the student is saying you never pay attention to what he or she says or that ''You embarrassed me in front of the class.'' Even in apparently clear-cut cases, you'll see conflicting opinions getting in the way of a solution. Remember, the first step in solving a problem is to define it. And discipline problems need two identifications: yours and the student's. That's why your major concern is: Who sees what — and why?

A Strategic Position Which Is A Benefit To All

Using this strategic position technique has obvious benefits for you and your students alike. It will save you time. It will help you home in on the right problem or problems rather than work on the wrong areas because of your perspective. It will also help you to decide upon an approach, and prevent your saying and doing things you'll be sorry for later. Looking at both viewpoints will keep you from making one of the biggest mistakes of all — prejudging.

As managers of classrooms, we are only as good as the input we receive. When we try to guess how students are thinking, we are doing just that — guessing. And we will usually guess wrong. It's not surprising, for prejudgments usually are wrong. Our professional task is not to guess, but to discover.

Finding out who sees what and why prevents misdirection, curtails wasted effort, and eliminates a great deal of frustration for teachers and students alike. It facilitates solving the whole problem rather than only part of it. Unfortunately, too often we think the situation is so obvious that there couldn't possibly be two sides. If we realize that there are usually two sides to every discipline problem, and then take precise action steps to determine the various viewpoints in every discipline situation, we'll gain the knowledge needed to begin dealing with the situation effectively. Without adopting such a teacher strategic action, we are likely to run in circles. Worse, we are apt to make the same moves and experience the same failures again and again without knowing why. When this happens, the despair of failure alone can cause us to be ineffective.

Summary

Neither students nor teachers can solve a problem unless they know they have one. Part of this knowledge comes through joint identification of problems. And because we are all humans who see things through our own eyes, we usually perceive things differently. That's why a teacher needs to search out the student's side in any problem situation.

Failure to discover this difference in perception can cause other problems. For instance, when we refer students to a counselor or principal, do we know what often happens? We tell the counselor or principal one story. Then, the student tells another. The stories don't match. What should these colleagues do? How should they proceed? If they support the student, they lose the teacher's respect. If they support the teacher, they lose the student's respect. Worse, the problem is left to fester.

As professional educators, we must not put students, colleagues, or ourselves in such a vulnerable position. We won't, if we try to find out how students perceive the problem and encourage administrators to do the same. Then we will gain the information needed for solving problems and changing behavior. We can hope to recognize the need for such input before actions are taken or punishments imposed. That's why getting both viewpoints — finding out who sees what and why — must be our first strategic action step in solving discipline problems.

PART FOUR

ALWAYS SEPARATE ATTITUDE AND BEHAVIOR

Strategic Action Rationale: Attitude and behavior are two separate human responses. If a teacher is getting the desired behavior, and reprimands attitude, he or she may no longer get the desired behavior.

If there are any two things that perplex and even anger teachers, they are student attitude and student behavior. We are concerned that students do what we tell them to do when we tell them to do it — as well as with the manner in which they do it. This latter concern includes how quickly they respond to our commands and how they look and act when they do.

When we tell a student to pick something up off the floor, we expect him or her to do it now — in an understanding, gracious, and respectful way. If the student is not quick to obey, we are likely to be quick with a reprisal. Too, if the student even appears to want to say something unfavorable, his or her attitude toward our command is most likely to stir our anger and initiate the thought of counseling, reprimand, or punishment. It is these little incidents that cause much of the distasteful part of teaching — and cause us to take the wrong strategic actions. Most certainly, attitudes cause some teachers more trouble than others; yet they touch us all. Without doubt, if we could somehow take these kinds of experiences out of our relationships with students, teaching would be more enjoyable to us all.

Two Separate Responses

There is a key to minimizing these kinds of bad situations. However, a teacher must first be able to separate student behavior from attitude and respond differently to each.

Attitude and behavior are two different student responses — and should be reacted to separately by a teacher. Demanding or expecting both to improve simultaneously may not even be realistic. Every teacher I have known who demanded that student attitude and behavior responses match either created a discipline situation where none existed, or made a bad situation worse.

The First Objective Is Behavior

Remember, the appropriate behavior is your primary desire. If you tell a child to do something and he or she begins a movement in that direction, regardless of how slowly or with what degree of reluctance, be satisfied with the behavior — for the time being. There are several reasons why the behavior alone should be satisfying enough.

Put yourself in the position of receiving a command, or even a demand. Let's say that your department head asks you to do something you don't want to do. At the moment you begin "obeying the order," you may experience many emotions. These emotions may range from anger to degradation. In fact, one word added to the order by your superior may bring an explosion. We've all had these experiences — and they are quite normal.

Students experience the same feelings — and they must be allowed. The important issue here is that there is movement in the direction of the command. Sometimes, to expect a student not to pout, sulk, or get angry when told to do something is simply unrealistic. If a teacher confuses the attitude with the behavior, a strategic action mistake may be made.

Often, teachers cannot accept the fact that, at this point, getting the behavior is the most important aspect of leadership. The probability exists that in certain situations — whether it be a department head making a request of a teacher, or a teacher directing a child — we may not get *both* a favorable behavior and a favorable attitude response at the same time. In fact, if we do get such a response, it may be insincere. It may even be abnormal. I'm not saying that the attitude displayed is not important, nor that it should not be dealt with. But this is neither the time nor the place to deal with it — if we intend to be the agents of change in a student's life.

It should also be noted that attitude can easily be misread. A misinterpretation of a student's attitude followed by a reprimand, when the student thinks he or she is complying with the teacher's request, can cause problems. It's the thing that causes students to say, "Why should I? If the teacher doesn't like *how I do it,* I get in trouble anyway." Total insubordination is often the final result when children have such feelings. In truth, when a teacher gets a positive action response in behavior and not in attitude, he or she can easily make a neutral situation negative by adding reprimand to the issue of attitude. Remember, just asking a kid to do something does not mean he or she has to jump up and down with joy while complying with your request. That's why your professional strategic action must separate attitude and behavior. And behavior is the primary consideration. Attitude is the secondary desire. But if you criticize attitude when you're getting the desired behavior, you may end up getting neither the desired behavior nor the desired attitude.

Summary

The teacher must fully recognize the importance of both behavior and attitude. Yet, at times, these two responses must be separated in our work when disciplining students. Our problems often result when we make issues of both at the same time. Sometimes, confrontations about attitudes result in students not even responding with behavior — and then we have real problems. Getting the behavior is the more significant of the two in the early stages of effecting change. In addition, nine times out of ten, when the behavior changes, the attitude change will follow. That's a fact.

If a conflict appears obvious, wait until later to counsel a student about attitude. Realize it is often the many emotions the student experienced at the time of the correction or reprimand that cause him or her to respond negatively. Too, as students comply with teacher requests, they are often forced to respond with a negative attitude to "save face" in the presence of their peers. In truth, it may be abnormal for a student to jump up with a smiling face and a "yes" on his or her lips every time he or she is told to do something. People simply don't react in this manner. And if they did, you might regard them as smart alecks.

There are receptive times to show students how their attitudes toward what they did ruined the effort they extended. These are the times to counsel students regarding the importance of attitude in the world of work and in life. These are the times to illustrate how others failed to appreciate their efforts or accept them because of a poor display of attitude, and how, in reality, a public display such as they revealed is only self-degrading.

The professional teacher must always treat attitude and behavior separately. When we try to put them together in times of stress, they will often refuse to merge. When this is the case, forcing them together will usually result in a teacher's having two kinds of problems rather than one.

PART FIVE

COUNSELING STUDENTS ABOUT ATTITUDES

Strategic Action Rationale: Counseling students about attitudes is a two-step process. Students must be prepared for discussion sessions rather than simply approached "cold turkey" for in-depth lessons regarding their attitude.

There's no doubt we all have our own definitions of good and bad attitudes. And there's no doubt regarding the importance of a good attitude in school as well as in the world of work. Good attitudes can open doors. They can even compensate for a lack of ability — and for good reason.

A worker can have all the talent in the world, but a poor attitude can negate every one of his or her abilities. Therefore, sheer ability is not everything. In fact, studies reveal that only fifteen percent of the people who lose or leave jobs do so because of a lack of ability. Eighty-five percent of all terminations are related to attitude. They're the result of an inability to get along with other people — colleagues, customers, managers, or others. Students need to know these facts. Our task in the classroom is to manage and develop student attitudes. Here are some "dos and don'ts" relative to the task.

First, as I've said before, don't talk to students about *attitude* when you're talking about the behavior. Separate the two characteristics. Second, don't send students with poor attitudes to see someone else unless you're counseling these students too. Such a stance indicates teacher inability to cope with the problem and implies rejection of the student — not just the attitude. Third, don't expect these students to change overnight. They won't. Fourth, recognize that you must be willing to give them your time outside class to resolve the problem. Fifth, resolve to ask and question, but not tell. Remember, you can't impose your truths upon these students and be effective. However, you can share your beliefs — and there's a big difference between these two teacher actions.

When you begin to counsel attitudes, plant seeds rather than trees. Don't try to have any lengthy conversation until you think a student is ready to listen. Counseling students about attitudes is a two-step processs. First, students must be prepared for lengthy talks. Until they are, plant one seed at a time by saying, "You seem unhappy," or "Things seem to be working against you." It's the seed planting of an objective truth that will get them thinking and prepare them for later counseling.

When you do have a long talk, use the comparison technique. It's very effective. Say, "You do the same work as others and never get any credit. Do you know why? It's this thing called attitude." Relate that classmates may not want to comply with every teacher request either. However, point out that they don't wear their displeasure on their sleeves and offend by their attitudes.

When counseling, don't talk about right and wrong. Too many students who are discipline problems have heard this approach before, time and time again. Rather, talk about dumb and smart — and the law of averages. They understand and relate to these terms more easily. Say, "It's dumb to act the way you do and get in trouble. It's not smart. Too, the law of averages says if you act in bad ways and get away with it ten times, eventually somebody is going to get mad. So the law of averages will catch up with you and get you in trouble.''

Summary

We know that we can't solve every problem for students. We can only help them solve their problems. The student with a bad attitude is a living testament to this reality. Ours is a responsibility to share and guide, not demand or impose. Telling won't change an attitude. Helping students discover what works for and against them holds the best chance for success.

We know counseling students about attitudes takes time. Improvement can't be achieved in one or two sessions. We must be willing to give this student our time and counsel. This is a problem that cannot and will not be resolved on class time. Likewise, setbacks are likely along the way. Yet, if we do nothing, we allow the perpetuation of a trait which may defeat even our best students for the rest of their lives. Therefore, the strategic action which offers the highest probability of success when changing attitudes involves preparing students for counseling sessions — and these sessions must include sharing your truths rather than forcing them upon students.

PART SIX

NEVER ASK WHY... ASK WHAT

Strategic Action Rationale: Asking a student* what *he or she did and* what *he or she is going to do about it is a strategic action which has a better chance of changing behavior than asking a student* why *he or she misbehaved.

A teacher can't minimize the importance of the word ''why'' as an educational tool. It's almost a synonym for the word ''learning.'' But when it comes to relating to and changing misbehavior, there are countless times when ''what'' is much more important and effective than ''why.''

Because the word ''why'' is such a dominating one in the life of a teacher, we often use it at the wrong times and in the wrong places. This is especially true in discipline situations. We are naturally concerned with the causes or reasons behind a child's misbehavior. Maybe that's one reason we say to a student, ''Why did you say that?'' or ''Why would you do a thing like that?'' In truth, we would be much more successful if we would ask questions beginning with ''what'' in all discipline situations. As a strategic action, a teacher can make asking ''what'' a rule and asking ''why'' a rule violation in changing misbehavior.

The Negative Effect Of "Why"

Asking ''why'' when correcting behavior can produce negative responses which range from no response to shallow answers. It can also produce attitudes ranging from defensiveness to belligerence. That's the reason we need to know about ''why'' and ''what'' and how they affect student behavior.

First, we all recognize that no technique will work for every teacher in *all* situations. Yet, some techniques have a sound educational basis while others do not. For instance, belittling or hitting a student may quiet the student, but could never be justified professionally. Too, some techniques do have a higher probability of success than others and, without doubt, some of the most effective techniques are extremely simple. I say this because teachers use both ''why'' and ''what'' daily. Though both are simple words by themselves, one should never believe for a moment they are not complex in their ability to effect change in student behavior.

In discipline situations, remember that ''what'' is a positive, and ''why'' is a negative. We cannot motivate students in behavior situations as we do in academic ones. ''Why'' is a stimulant in an academic situation. However — if a student cheats on a test, is late to class, talks back, throws something on the floor, or is being disruptive — asking the student ''why'' can elicit a negative response, and is not a motivating action insofar as changing his or her behavior is concerned.

Losing The Real Issue

Students may not know ''why'' they talk continually, bully classmates, or are late to class. Equally important, when people do things they are not proud of, they often can't face the question of ''why'' at that time. Even though a student may not be able to deal with ''why'' upon confrontation, however, he or she may *feel compelled* to give an answer — any answer. We all do this, for we do feel we must answer for our behavior, as well as possess self-control to the point that we can explain ourselves. Unfortunately, sometimes we can't explain ourselves. For instance, it is difficult for a child to explain ''why'' he or she knocked a book on the floor. Therefore, when we ask ''why,'' we should not be surprised at the answer we receive.

When a teacher insists upon asking ''why'' and getting an answer, the ''why'' *rather than the misbehavior* becomes the issue. Remember, as the class waits and watches, the behavior — not the reason for it — is the issue. If we forget this fact, we may never be successful in changing student behavior — immediately or permanently. Rather, we may perpetuate the offering of excuses and, in many ways, trivialize or reinforce the misbehavior. To maintain self-respect and avoid self-degradation, the student simply persists in the behavior. That's a fact. This applies to teachers as well. When confronted with ''why'' they have certain class rules or ''why'' they will not support a new idea, we've all seen teachers persistently cling to their actions and beliefs simply to save face. That's our humanness. It's also the reason why it's not always wise to confront anybody with ''why'' at certain times. That is, it's not if we want to change a behavior.

Some teachers will even ask a student why he or she is misbehaving when they already know the answer. That's a real professional mistake. Time and again, we know hyperactivity or a low self-concept lies at the root of the misbehavior. Yet, we ask a student to tell us ''why'' — knowing all the time we won't get the real reasons. We may become part of the problem when we choose such a course of action. Therefore, our strategic action should be to ask ''what.'' Simply say, ''What did you do?'' Then ask, ''What are you going to do about it?'' Ask both questions in quick succession. Do *not* wait for an answer to the first question before asking the second. A child will usually respond, ''I dropped a book, I'll pick it up.'' That's because ''what'' gives the child a chance to respond rationally. It also asks him or her to take a positive course of action. Asking ''why'' does neither. This simple tip will work for you hundreds of times each year.

Summary

Using ''what'' is usually more effective than ''why'' in discipline situations. It is most effective when used as a simply stated question — without even a hint of reprimand, sarcasm, or disdain. Remember, it is offered to motivate appropriate behavior.

Always recognize behavior as the primary issue. Ask simply: ''What did you do?'' and ''What are you going to do about it?'' These two questions place emphasis on the real issue and establish the responsibility for misbehavior where it should be — with the student. This strategic action also enables a student to answer with a course of action or a solution. Even if a student refuses to acknowledge ''what'' he or she did or ''what'' he or she is going to do about it, asking ''why'' is pointless.

Such questions as ''Why were you late?'' only bring on answers like ''Because my mother didn't wake me up.'' Asking ''Why did you fail?'' brings excuses such as ''I didn't understand,'' and ''Why were you talking?'' elicits ''Because she was talking to me.'' From this point, teacher action can become negative and ineffective, and can make a big problem out of a little one. Using ''what'' rather than ''why'' also gives us room to operate after the student response. Then, we are on the road to effecting change and building relationships with students in the process. And that's what we are trying to do. We will, if we ask ''what'' more often in discipline situations — and ask ''why'' a lot less.

PART SEVEN

THE PEOPLE PRIORITIES

Strategic Action Rationale: Students are attempting to meet these seven needs in and out of the classroom and school via either appropriate or inappropriate behavior.

It's not easy to make children want to learn, be responsible, and behave as they know they should. Yet, to be unable to do so forfeits our ability to teach — regardless of how much academic knowledge we possess. Even if we teach for a lifetime, we may find ourselves working just as hard trying to get students to behave at the end of our careers as we did in the beginning. One would think that once motivational behavioral techniques and skills were mastered, they would become easy, routine tasks for any teacher. But it doesn't work that way. That's why we need to understand and master the primary motivators. They work, and for good reason. It's through attainment of these needs that students are motivated to strive to reach personal goals.

The Seven Motivators

There are seven basic human motivators. I call them people priorities because they represent what is important to people. These motivators can be used with every student you teach. So effective are they that businesses use one or more of these needs to motivate people to purchase every product that has ever been made. If you think not, read the newspaper or watch television tonight. See how many of these motivators are used in each advertisement. You may be amazed. And, you'll probably see the need to apply them to your efforts to motivate pupils to exhibit appropriate behavior in the classroom. These seven motivators are: personal gain, prestige, pleasure, security, convenience, imitation, and the desire to avoid fear.

A close look might reveal that if we aren't using these individual motivators, many of the things we are doing to motivate students toward proper behavior may be counterproductive. Let's take a look at each motivator to see if our efforts are directed toward stimulating students in the classroom — or turning them off.

Personal Gain...Prestige...Pleasure...Security

Personal gain is the primary motivator of most human beings. The difficulty arises from the fact that what is considered a personal gain by one person isn't a gain for another. That's why the primary question, "What's in learning and behaving for me?" must be answered individually for each student. This, of course, means a teacher can't say, "Do this for me," or "I need you to do this," in the classroom. If we do, our efforts may cancel motivation.

Prestige is also a behavior and learning motivator. Remember, learning and behavior are personal. The prestige motive helps students gain recognition, win approval, and feel important. If we put students down or make them feel insignificant in any way, we may be inadvertently denying the prestige motivator. Likewise, if we don't give recognition for success, we can't use the prestige motivator effectively.

Pleasure is among the strongest motivators. Ask yourself, "How many things do I do, or buy, as a result of this one motivator?" People want to have fun. Students are not the exception to this reality. Often, we would much rather relax or play than work. If we think school isn't supposed to be fun, then our motivational efforts may be defeated by this one prejudiced belief. Any teacher who believes that acquiring knowledge and behaving appropriately aren't pleasurable is in the wrong profession.

Security is also a motivator. Students, like anyone else, want safety and like the strength and peace of mind that come from being secure. So, if we frighten students or make threats concerning grades or behavior, the insecurity we produce may be counterproductive to motivation.

Convenience...Imitation...Avoiding Fear

Everyone wants things to be easy. That's why convenience is a motivator. The fast food industry has made a fortune meeting this need. And we should make use of this motivator by making learning as easy and convenient as possible. One thing is certain — if we think a long or hard assignment or complex daily rules stimulate students, we are mistaken. Remember, learning and behavior may be hard, but a teacher had better be careful about purposely making either look hard — or making it more convenient for students to disobey than to obey.

Imitation is keeping up with peers, following the crowd, and imitating one's heroes. Like it or not, students will be more like the adults in their lives than not. This is one of the reasons teachers are so influential — and why we must be models to young people. If we are cold, sarcastic, or intolerant, students may learn the wrong lessons from us.

Finally, the desire to avoid fear motivates. This motivator is probably the one we use the most but should use the least. If we're making school a fearful place for students, we're using a destructive practice to gain results. And the problem student is likely to choose flight or fight to avoid fear. This is the reason some kids won't try, won't participate in class discussions, or get sick on test days.

Summary

These seven motivators are vital teaching tools which shouldn't be left out of our repertoire of discipline skills. That's why we must examine what we are saying and doing to get some kids to behave in acceptable ways. It just may be that we are inadvertently cancelling our intentions.

When something goes wrong or isn't going as we think it should, then we need to look at how we are trying to get students to change their behavior. And our motivation plan must not be directed solely toward group teaching. Without reservation, it also needs to be individual, because the motivators are uniquely individual. That means that, to motivate students, we need more private talks and fewer class discussions about an individual student's misbehavior.

We must be more concerned with being individual learning leaders for each student than with being mass psychologists. We must confer privately with students to gain insight and ask questions. We must search for relevancy and look for clues to motivate each child. Once an individual student's need is discovered, we must try to fill it. We are not robots applying techniques to a roomful of students, but professionals concerned with the dignity of each human being. Difficult? Yes, of course. But herein lies the challenge and the reward for every one of us who has ever stepped into a classroom. That's why we should use these seven people priorities in our professional strategic action to motivate children to demonstrate appropriate attitudes and behavior in the classroom. Make no mistake, these motivators work.

PART EIGHT

KEEPING THE RESPONSIBILITY FOR MISBEHAVIOR WITH THE STUDENT

Strategic Action Rationale: Because of a need for power and control in the classroom, a teacher's action may diminish students' responsibility for their own behavior and, therefore, decrease the successful teaching of self-discipline as well as hinder problem solving.

There's no denying that a teacher is responsible for everything that happens in the classroom. If our students are unruly or misbehave in the halls, auditorium, or cafeteria, it's our responsibility to see that they behave properly in these places. Yet, the truth of the matter is that we often assume *too much* responsibility for children. I say that because, after all, kids are responsible too. That's why we must make sure that neither our method of teaching appropriate behavior nor our discipline techniques are putting all the responsibility for appropriate behavior on us — and none on kids.

Class Rules Don't Necessarily Teach Self-Discipline

Perspective should tell us that we can't *make* kids behave. That is, we can't unless we intend to watch them continuously as well as make all their personal decisions for them. That's why a teacher can't legislate discipline in the classroom. In truth, discipline can't be legislated in life. Our traffic laws, especially the 55 m.p.h. speed laws, attest to this fact. We can make all the class rules and regulations we want — and we know that some students will break them even when the majority obeys.

Experience should also tell us that the best strategic action, insofar as discipline is concerned, promotes self-discipline. That's why our efforts to manage a roomful of students should lean heavily on the rationale for teaching appropriate behavior — rather than focusing primarily on making rules or punishing kids if they don't behave properly. In many ways, leaning heavily on punishments takes responsibility for behaving away from students. Such things as decision making and questions of right and wrong can get clouded by "what the teacher is doing to me" and "It's okay to misbehave — if you don't get caught."

Once teachers understand this reality, they can move more easily to taking strategic action which gives kids *more responsibility* for their behavior. Part of our success in doing so has a great deal to do with our techniques. And our techniques can be altered by accepting the fact that kids, like all other human beings, want some measure of control over their own lives. Herein lies a valuable clue for knowing how to teach students successfully to reveal more self-discipline — and learn from their experiences.

Tell Students, "I Don't Decide; Your Behavior Tells Me What I Must Do."

Here's a strategic action that is highly effective in dealing with students — individually and collectively. This technique utilizes individual pressure — and a degree of peer pressure. First, drop all pretenses that you are the holder of all power, the boss, and totally responsible for what students do or do not do. Make sure they know they're never playing a game with you when they misbehave. Rather, they're playing a game with themselves. It's their life, not yours. You care, but you cannot control them. Most important, tell students you don't want to control them.

Then, tell students they hold the power to determine the degree of their freedom. It's their mature use of power to discipline themselves which determines the degree. Say, *"I don't make the rules in this class. I don't decide what you can and can't do."* Tell students, *"I'm the teacher — and responsible for all of you. But your behavior tells me what I can and can't allow you to do. Your behavior tells me what rules to make — and which ones aren't necessary. Some young people can have great latitude while others can't. But in every case — it's you who tell me what to do. In truth, when you misbehave, you are asking me to do something. So don't get mad when I must correct you — or when I make a rule. You told me to correct you, or make the rule, through your behavior."*

This stance puts the responsibility for behavior where it belongs — on the student. Equally important, it doesn't take any authority *away* from a teacher. It doesn't make a teacher look mean, unfair, uncaring, or out of control. In addition, this strategic action doesn't make a teacher create rules and regulations for the majority in order to cover the minority. Rather, it allows a teacher to place limitations on the few who misuse their responsibility. Also, this one benefit is an absolute necessity in gaining and keeping the respect of those students who do display self-discipline and deserve more freedom.

Summary

It's improbable that students will ever really accept responsibility for their own behavior — unless we make them responsible. And part of this responsibility comes from placing the emphasis on *what they do* rather than *what we're going to do* when they misbehave.

Students also need to be taught that, as in life, how other people perceive them does count. For instance, if others, including the teacher, believe they are being discourteous or infringing on the rights of others, this is the issue. And they need to know that their nonverbal behavior is as powerful as their verbal behavior. Stares, moans, groans, and facial expressions should be subject to self-discipline.

Make sure students know that they are always sending messages to a teacher. These messages tell a teacher how they feel — and tell what teachers can and can't do in the classroom insofar as freedom is concerned. They reveal how much supervision is needed. And as professional educators, we only respond to what our students tell us. The choice is theirs. Part of teaching self-discipline is to begin letting students be responsible for the choices they make. That's why adopting this strategic action is essential to teaching self-discipline and, therefore, cutting down on the number of misbehaviors we must handle each day. This is vital because all studies show that it's not the misbehavior that causes teacher stress and burnout — it is the *frequency* of *small, continually repeated* misbehaviors that causes us the greatest frustrations.

PART NINE

TOUCH THE HURT

Strategic Action Rationale: A teacher must diagnose, relate the cause and effect of misbehavior specifically rather than generally, and take action in a professional, caring, and direct way to resolve discipline problems.

Make no mistake: Our human condition often makes us avoiders of hurt. If something is painful for us to think about or deal with, we may pretend it isn't happening. Certainly, it's more common than uncommon to fear or refuse to deal with it openly. That's why we need to learn to acquire the skills and employ the professional strategic action necessary to touch the hurt we witness before the pain gets out of control. If we don't, we shall never really help students resolve difficulties. Rather, we may be consumed by discipline problems, and they may render us ineffective as professional educators.

Getting To The Issue

Certainly, most of us have been in a situation — academic or discipline — that we wished would go away. We need to recognize this fact, for it is often our failure to face the facts in an academic situation which results in a discipline problem. In the hope that the problem will disappear, we sometimes go along ignoring the facts as they keep presenting themselves. A child isn't listening, isn't passing tests, isn't participating in class, or someone is opposing our every action, and we hope everything will "work itself out." In the beginning, we choose to do nothing. In the end, we find we can do nothing. We have allowed the situation to deteriorate because we weren't *willing or able* to touch the hurt for a wide variety of reasons, including not wanting to take the time or not wanting to face parents. Our professional perspective should tell us how grave a mistake we have made. If we look to other professionals, we can see how serious this situation can be — for us, our students, and the entire school.

If someone breaks his or her leg, does a doctor choose to do nothing in order to avoid further hurting the leg? Of course not. Neither does the doctor choose to treat the arm to avoid touching the injured leg. Yet, this is similar to what we often do in education. When we have a personality conflict with a student, we may criticize his or her attitude rather than deal with the real issues. If an entire class fails our test, we may say they didn't study. We may even skirt the real issues in academic performance. Too often, we tell parents that their child "will be okay in time," or that "things will all work out" when we have strong evidence to the contrary. And that's the problem. We don't touch the hurt where the pain is — and nothing gets resolved.

Like the doctor, we must deal with the issues directly. A doctor can't set a broken leg without touching it. The doctor knows it will hurt. His or her responsibility is to touch in a caring way and cause as little pain as possible in the process. Our responsibility as professional educators is the same — before a situation, academic or behavioral, moves beyond our control.

A Common Mistake

Unfortunately, many people were taught as children to avoid issues. It was part of their upbringing. We may have learned it was best to keep problems buried within ourselves, even if doing so meant hurting ourselves. Telling adults about our problems only brought more problems. So we learned to make choices. We decided that the best rule for survival was not to touch our own hurts — much less those of others. Mother would say, "If you can't get along with Johnny, don't play with him."

If we have managed to come to adulthood through this system of ignoring our hurts, then we may function the same way as adults. This presents a formidable problem — especially if we are in a position of working with people. Such is certainly the case for teachers.

We all should recognize that there is something we can do. We can change this strategic action approach. Admittedly, this is a most difficult thing to do. We may not know how to go about changing, much less approaching our hurt, and those of the children we teach, in a caring way. But if we don't act on our determination to make alterations, then we might as well not have found out change was necessary. Change is the most painful thing we humans take part in — but if we don't change, we forfeit real living for dull existence, and our ability to help children is minimal, at best. This is hardly a choice to be pursued.

When we decide to touch the hurt as professional teachers, we need only remember three things. First, we need to make sure we are dealing with the real issues in a professional rather than a petty way. We cannot allow ourselves any "game playing" here — for this is a serious business. Second, we need to deal quickly and honestly with problems rather than let them grow. Third, we need to deal with the hurts of students in a caring way, trying to cause the least amount of hurt in the healing process. This is our challenge as professional teachers. It is one we cannot avoid.

Summary

The problems of students will not dissolve like dew on a morning leaf. Like people who do not like to go to the dentist for fear of pain, teachers do not look forward to meeting issues head-on. People often delay going to the doctor or dentist until the pain of not going is greater than the anticipated pain of going. Similarly, we often delay dealing specifically, directly, and totally with a discipline problem. That's a strategic action mistake.

Yet, dealing with the hurt often causes less pain than anticipated. Indeed, it may cause less pain than all the things we usually do to avoid it. Above all, recognize that our professional position dictates that we treat issues at their source. Our responsibility is to touch the hurt in a caring way — remembering that some of the hurt may have to do with us.

We humans too often function from our reluctance, when we ought to be functioning from our love. The times when we will be rebuffed for offering love are so few that they are hardly worth mentioning. This is particularly true in the teacher-student-parent relationship. Even when it appears that a child is refusing our love, more than likely that child is merely hiding his or her surprise. We would all do better as teachers if we could give students many more such surprises, and adopt the professional strategic action of touching the hurt quickly in a gentle and caring way.

PART TEN

CONFRONTING

Strategic Action Rationale: Confronting is a prerequisite for handling misbehavior, but it must be achieved from a stance of caring and consideration rather than anger or hate — or negative student responses become the probability.

In some matters there is almost always a contradiction between what we say we believe and what we actually do. So it is with confrontation. All our lives we have been taught that honesty is the best policy. Indeed, we say that we believe honesty *is always* the best course of action. Yet, when it comes to confronting another person about something wrong or something we dislike, we can rationalize not confronting that person as the caring and wise thing to do. There may be many good reasons why we choose this course. Yet, as professional educators, we still need to look at them.

A Difficult Move

None can deny that confronting effectively is a difficult thing to do. Certainly, it's easier to write about it than to do it. In the first place, many of our experiences with confronting or being confronted may have been bad ones. That's why we can think of all kinds of reasons not to confront. When we feel the need and urge, therefore, all kinds of personal emotions are brought into play. One is fear that confronting will just cause additional problems. Also, perhaps we don't know how to confront, can't find the right time and place, don't want to take the time, or don't really care enough to confront.

Regardless, if teachers cannot and will not perfect the art of confrontation, they will have difficulty handling discipline problems. The plain truth is that if we can't confront successfully, we can't always help students. Confrontation is often the best course of action. Sometimes, it's the only one.

Of course, there are different kinds of confrontations. Obviously, a duel with swords is one kind. Honest, open, and gentle exchange of differences is quite another. One is a war; the other is not — and there are few situations in our classrooms that call for "wars." Unfortunately, we often think of confrontation in discipline situations as being just that — a war. Once we eliminate this myth from our minds, we can begin learning to use confrontation as a valuable strategic action tool. If we still question the wisdom of confronting, we should ask ourselves whether the decision not to confront can be called a genuine solution or just a weak avoidance.

A Way To Begin

Confronting may not be something we like to do, but it is something we have to do. And we need to do it well. Realize that there is no such thing as the right time and place — but there may be the wrong time and place. That's why, above all, public confrontation should be avoided. When you know you must confront, be aware that people don't confront people or things that they don't care about — quite the contrary. Herein lies the key to your attitude, approach, and action when confronting students.

First, *always* talk about caring when you confront. Convey the fact that problems don't get resolved unless they are talked out. And be sure you tell the student that you know he or she can handle the truth of your thinking better than the deceit of your saying nothing. Let the student absorb what you are saying — and never demand a response. Often, it's wise to make your first discussion short. But always make plans to talk again soon. And never, under any circumstances, let the matter hang for days before you talk again. As a general rule, the younger the student, the shorter the space between discussions.

There is one mistake commonly made in confronting. That's talking about everything *but* the real hardcore subject that brought you to the confrontation. Remember, you must touch the hurt. Don't talk around the issue. If you do, people will know that you're doing so — and they'll resent it. Just approach the issue in a gentle, caring, and considerate way. I have found from experience that you can confront students about almost anything if students know you like and care about them. On the other hand, it's difficult to confront students about anything at all if they think you dislike, disapprove, or don't care about them *as people.* That's why you must lay a caring foundation. It's as important to you as it is to the student you are confronting. After all, love is the base for human acceptance. And that's not surprising. Of all the emotions, it's one we cannot seem to live without.

Summary

We need to develop the skill to confront and make it a part of our strategic action. We can, if we look upon confrontation as an act of caring rather than an act of hate. This professional attitude alone will guide our action. It will determine what we say and how we say it. It will also guarantee that we address the real issue rather than talk around it. After all, we can't convince anyone that we care by playing games.

Too, confronting must be private, and, furthermore, it must remain confidential. That's the only way future caring confrontations are possible. Students don't want to hear how successfully a teacher confronted another student for fear that their own future confrontations with that teacher will be made public.

In truth, our reluctance to confront may say something about how we feel about being confronted ourselves. That's because when we decide to confront, we may also have to admit to certain faults in ourselves. Too, some change may be due on our part. As we speak, we may find the other person has some disclosures to make as well. And if we can allow them, we'll find it quite a disarming and healing move.

Remember, though our classrooms may be wonderful places, we do not reside in Utopia. We spend our days in schools where the population density is probably the highest in town. That's why we always have people problems. We can't leave problems alone and expect to help students or get the work of the school accomplished. Our success can come only through genuine solution. It will never result from avoidance. That's why we need to learn how to confront in a caring way. Confronting is a vital strategic action necessary to solve discipline problems.

PART ELEVEN

TWO VITAL FORMS OF COMMUNICATION

Strategic Action Rationale: Both verbal and nonverbal communication are powerful. However, if the two contradict each other, nonverbal communication is the more powerful. In addition, nonverbal communication can cause as many problems between people as verbal communication.

When it comes to classroom communication, a teacher must never forget that we are always communicating, whether we are speaking or not. Remember, there are two kinds of communication — verbal and nonverbal. One uses words, and the other has been called the language of the sensitive. We are senders and receivers of both types of communication. That means all our communication efforts are a two-way street. And both types of communication reinforce, complement, accent, and help each other. They can also contradict each other. We should all realize that a teacher needs to know and understand these realities regarding verbal and nonverbal communication. Yet, there is more we should know about both.

When verbal and nonverbal communication conflict, they place students in a bind. Worse, the receiver of communication usually accepts the nonverbal communication and rejects the verbal when the two conflict. This fact is vital to teachers — especially in handling discipline situations. It gives us important clues for communicating with students. It also gives us important clues regarding the efforts of our students to communicate with us.

Clues For Teacher Action

Tests conducted on nonverbal communication indicate that teachers who are evaluated as good teachers perceive nonverbal communications from students better than others do. Tests also show that these teachers send better nonverbal clues to students. That's why we need to understand nonverbal communication. We can't teach without communicating. And a teacher is always communicating.

Students communicate with us nonverbally in many ways. If we are perceptive receivers of nonverbal communication, we will pick up on these clues. Then, we will change our strategic approach and action to make sure we are communicating. For instance, when we lose the attention of a class, students are telling us something. Likewise, whispering, gazing out the window, reading other materials, playing with objects, and passing notes are forms of nonverbal communication which tell us a teaching adjustment on our part is necessary. Too, when we ask a question and a student avoids eye contact with us, the nonverbal clues should tell us the student may not be prepared.

We also send nonverbal clues to students regarding behavior; we can be sure the majority will respond to these clues. Silence is a technique used often. So is the hard stare which tells students we have had enough and mean business.

We also communicate nonverbally to students when we act distressed or tired. The most common adult nonverbal communication is the headache. Sudden shifts in voice, tone, and pitch, and changing one's pace to hurried action are nonverbal communications. All these forms of nonverbal communication are important to us and to students when it comes to discipline — especially when we realize that it's the nonverbal that's accepted when the verbal and the nonverbal conflict. Then, our well-intended words may never be heard because our actions communicate a stronger message.

When You Receive...React

Teachers need to be aware that students are very good nonverbal communicators. We also need to realize that younger and slower students may do a poor job of expressing themselves verbally. But they do give us good nonverbal clues. Because teachers are educated and prefer words, they often overlook nonverbal communication. For instance, we would never call a student dumb. But we may send that message nonverbally without intention.

Observation of ourselves and students is the only way we can learn to recognize nonverbal communication. That's why we should watch for many things that we and students do. For instance, gentle moments, touching, and gestures all give us clues to messages being sent. So do paling, sweating, blushing, and physical mannerisms. Likewise, foot movements, voice variations, facial expressions, laughter, and lip and mouth movements are nonverbal communications students send to us, and we send to them. Hesitation is one of the most common. When we send these communications, students will respond. When they send these communications to us, we should respond as well.

Nonverbal communication is always revealed in the eyes. Eyes, it seems, are always talking, and provide valuable clues. Normal eye contact means communication is open. When people look down, it often means rejection. Avoiding eye contact suggests that someone does not feel secure or included. The stare means dislike. All these clues provided by nonverbal communication can help make teaching and learning easier on both sides of the desk. That is, they can if we pick them up and respond.

Summary

Teachers are always communicating by word and movement. Without intention, we may be ignoring a student simply by avoiding eye contact. Even our silence is sending a message. That's why we need to weigh nonverbal and verbal acts equally.

There are many things, large and small, that we can do to set the tone of communication we want in our classrooms. We can greet students as they enter our classrooms. We can always make eye contact when listening. We can realize that how we communicate can make a big difference in how students function academically and personally. Their achievement and ability to learn are closely tied to the communication exchange they are experiencing. Both behavior and motivation are influenced by students' abilities to read our communication.

Sometimes, even with the best of teacher intentions, communication is misunderstood or misinterpreted. One of the ways to know how things are being received is to hear what we say and see what we do. We can pause occasionally to check ourselves out. If we just remember that people are always communicating, our mistakes will be fewer and our successes greater. And if we remember that the nonverbal can cancel the verbal, we will know that the clues children give us can help us be better communicators. Being a good nonverbal communicator is vital to the success of our strategic action with students who misbehave as well as with all students.

PART TWELVE

TECHNIQUES FOR LISTENING

Strategic Action Rationale: Listening techniques are vital to establishing rapport with students — and they are specific. They require a definite teacher attitude and three different, and distinct, techniques.

If there's a common complaint by students and teachers, it's that the other doesn't listen. Each has the same complaint and criticism of the other. That's why it's paradoxical that both teacher and student will claim emphatically that they do listen. It's important for teachers to understand listening as well as develop listening skills. Likewise, it's important to teach students these listening skills as well. This one strategic action can make you highly effective in establishing rapport with students and handling discipline problems when they arise.

Listen...And Learn

There are no ifs, ands, or buts about listening skills. They are specific. Listening requires a definite attitude which is reflected in three different strategic action techniques. These three techniques are vital factors in becoming a good listener as well as being perceived as one — and this brings up a vitally important point. Students must *believe* we are good listeners. If you will practice these strategic actions, I promise that few students will ever again charge you with not listening. On the contrary, students will count listening as one of your greatest strengths as a teacher.

The first listening necessity is obvious — and an absolute. You must stop whatever you are doing when you are spoken to. Look directly into the eyes of the student addressing you. Maintain this stance throughout the entire conversation. Never let your eyes wander. Remember, you can't continue to grade papers, look over the shoulder of the talker, correct a misbehaving student in the back of the room, or look at your watch, and have students think you are listening. They won't. Too often, this is exactly what teachers do. Then we say, "Go ahead, I can hear you," or "I can do this and listen to you too." No, we can't. At least, as far as students are concerned, we can't. Therefore, total attention with eye contact is the first strategic action you must employ.

Second, you must engage the talker physically. This strategic action skill is much more important than most people realize. It's easy and much more comfortable to disengage the talker, and that's exactly why students don't think we are listening to what they say. To engage the talker, lean forward from your desk or bend forward from your chair. When standing, lean your upper body slightly toward the talker. Never lean back when standing or while seated in a chair. Propping feet on a desk or chair is the worst thing you can do. Likewise, don't tap a pencil, play with a trinket, or display any physical mannerism. Rather, keep your body quiet, or your mannerisms will be perceived as disinterest or nonlistening. They will also be a distraction to your listening and the other person's talking. Leaning forward and maintaining eye contact are two of the most important strategic action listening skills you can master. But they are not enough.

Responsive Listening

Though eye contact and physical engagement are absolutes, one more strategic action skill is necessary in order for students to *really believe* you are listening. This final skill actually tells students you're listening. It gives students what they want from talking to you — attention and involvement. This strategic action listening skill is called *responsive listening.*

This skill is not easy to master. That's because, to use it, you must really listen. This means, of course, that you want to listen because you believe that students and what they say are important.

Responsive listening is *not* repeating or parroting what others say to you. Neither is it telling others how *you* feel or giving replies which are parallel to what the talker is saying. Quite the contrary, responsive listening is responding to *what you feel you heard the student say, or to how the student feels about what he or she is saying.* Therefore, you tie into the talker's words and feelings rather than your own, and respond accordingly.

For instance, if a student says, "Do we have to take the test today?" your reply should never be, "If you had studied, you would be ready." Rather, you might simply say, "Why do you ask?" or "Are you afraid that you're not ready for the test?" Without this kind of empathetic responsive listening, you may not be hearing messages correctly. The student's reply may surprise you. For instance, the reply might be, "No, tests just scare me."

It shouldn't take a teacher long, in thinking through most discipline conversations with students, to realize that we often fail to be responsive listeners. Rather, we are advice listeners, answer listeners, corrective listeners, detached listeners, and opinion listeners. Maybe that's why students say we misinterpret what they've said, or claim they've tried to talk to us, but we wouldn't listen. If we were responsive listeners first, maybe we could move more easily and effectively to advice giving, counseling, and supporting — and correcting later. One thing is certain, when we learn to be responsive listeners, students will believe that we are easy to talk to. Therefore, they will be more apt to communicate more easily and freely with us.

Summary

It's true. We can do two things at once. We *can actually* work and listen at the same time. The problem is we'll never convince anyone else that we can. Worse, we'll never be able to convince students talking to us that we don't consider what we're working on more important than they, what they need, and what they have to say. That's why every teacher must develop and practice strategic action listening skills.

Without such skills, we will keep hearing the same old complaint — "My teacher never listens." And we will keep the circle intact by saying, "Students never listen." Worse, both teachers and students will continue blaming each other for their woes. That's why this is one circle that needs breaking. And we can break it simply by giving students who talk to us our undivided attention, making physical contact, and being responsive listeners. The benefits to our reputation as teachers who care may be greater than we can ever imagine. That's because children feel pretty good about adults who listen to them. Without adopting a strategic action which includes listening, it's very unlikely that you will resolve many discipline problems or position yourself to teach self-discipline effectively.

PART THIRTEEN

KEYS TO EFFECTIVE LISTENING

Strategic Action Rationale: To achieve listening, we must overcome three specific blockages — instant evaluation, noncritical interference and plural inference — by responding to both the ideas and the feelings being expressed.

Unfortunately, many of us were never taught how to listen, nor have we really practiced the art. That's why listening skills cannot be underemphasized by devoting only one part of this book to this strategic action.

Studies reveal that seventy-five percent of our waking hours are spent communicating with people. Of this time, we are listening forty percent of the time. Couple these two statistics with the fact that we remember only fifty percent of what we hear immediately after we hear it and only twenty-five percent of it a few days later — and the practical need to listen is revealed.

The problem of listening is compounded by the fact that we can talk at an average rate of 125 words a minute. But we can listen (think) at a rate of over 1,000 words a minute. Therefore, while listening we can drift away from a speaker's words at a rate of 875 words per minute. Our effectiveness as teachers, especially when handling discipline problems, is influenced by these statistics. Yet, very few of us would say, "I'm a poor listener." However, many of us are — and so are many students.

Developing Specific Habits Can Make You A Competent Listener

There are many things a teacher can do to develop listening skills in discipline situations — and teach students to do so as well. For instance, you can resist the urge, and purposely limit your own talking. Remember, you can't effectively talk and listen at the same time. Also, you can try to *think* like the student talking. You'll understand and retain words and feelings better if you keep the student's point of view in mind. This, of course, is a prerequisite for responsive listening which we discussed earlier.

Asking questions can also help develop listening skills. If you don't understand or feel you may have missed a point, clear it up with a question — or request repetition. In discipline situations we often talk too much —

and don't want to listen. In fact, we don't *intend* to listen. Rather, we intend *to do all the talking.* This is where big problems begin.

Likewise, refrain from interruptions or from jumping in as soon as a student finishes a sentence. A pause, even a long pause, doesn't always mean a student has finished saying everything he or she wants to say. And in discipline situations, letting a child talk himself or herself out can almost always be very advantageous.

When you look directly at the student, always focus your mind on what the student is saying and feeling. Practice shutting off outside distractions. In conferences, take notes to help you remember important points. However, be selective in note taking. Trying to write down everything being said can result in your being left far behind or in retaining irrelevant details. Therefore, listen for ideas, not just words. You want to get the whole picture, not just isolated bits and pieces. Remember, your strategic action needs information. Therefore, you must gather every bit of information before you act.

You Must React To The Ideas And Feelings, Not To The Person

Your verbal response can also help you stay involved in a conversation and help others know you're listening as well. An occasional, "Yes ... I see" shows you're still with them. However, don't overdo this practice or use meaningless comments. Interjected responses must be sincere or they will have the opposite effect from what you intended.

While listening to explanations, turn off your own worries. This isn't always easy. Personal fears, concerns, problems — and work that is waiting for you — can keep you from listening effectively. These obstacles form a kind of "static" that can block out communications from students. Therefore, your worries may hamper your listening. Prepare remarks and questions in advance whenever possible. This frees your mind for better listening.

Above all, to be a good listener you must react to ideas and not just to the student speaking. Don't allow the manner in which a student speaks to irritate you. Such irritation can distract you totally, and you'll miss everything said. Too, don't argue mentally or allow yourself to jump to conclusions. Avoid making unwarranted assumptions about what the student is going to say. Finally, never mentally try to complete sentences for the student talking. All these actions prevent your listening because they distract you from what is actually being said. Make it a habit to use these techniques and you'll become a competent listener. You'll also have *all the information* you need to take action.

Summary

Remember, *instant evaluation, noncritical interference,* and *plural inference* are three blocks to listening. When we practice *instant evaluation,* we pass judgment too early, jump to conclusions, or assume that others think as we do. To avoid *noncritical interference,* we can listen with the intent to understand rather than to counter. And to avoid *plural inference,* we can always probe for details as well as ask "what" and "why."

A closed mind, lack of attention, wishful thinking, and semantics can also block listening. To avoid a closed mind in discipline situations, one must acquire a thirst for *complete information,* for it's the only cure for such a blockage. To keep our minds from wandering, we can listen with other senses in addition to hearing. Likewise, to avoid hearing only what we want to hear, we must stress objective listening. Words can cause semantic problems because certain words mean different things to different people. We must, therefore, listen beyond words. We must search for the message.

Finally, remember that excessive talking, fear, and lack of humility can block listening. And these are real problems for many teachers. That's because we often want to solve the problem for ourselves rather than for the student. Therefore, we must keep quiet to listen, control our fears, and overcome our own prejudice and arrogance at times. The teacher who cannot listen may never know students or discover the real problem in discipline situations. That's why the art of listening is a skill we must perfect as a part of our professional strategic action.

PART FOURTEEN

SHARING THE RESPONSIBILITY WITH PARENTS

Strategic Action Rationale: Unless a teacher shares problem solving with parents, he or she has not only overlooked an important resource, but has also moved beyond his or her authority and responsibility as an educator.

Sometimes teachers assume too much responsibility. Trying to be the sole resolver of all the academic, behavior, and attitude problems of our students is a good example. Though we are responsible for these things, so are parents. That's why we need to share responsibility with them. Not only might our peace of mind be greatly improved, but we might also find that sharing the responsibility with parents gives better results than assuming all the responsibility ourselves. The question is: Why don't we involve parents more than we do?

A Prejudgment

Some teachers might respond that they don't have time to contact parents. Many may be afraid, or think parents don't want to be — or will refuse to be — involved. Others may believe that parents don't care. I've heard teachers say, "I don't understand parents — none responded to the progress report I sent home," then add, "Do you know what my parents would have done if they had received a letter from a teacher?"

I don't pretend to know what each of our parents would have done under similar circumstances. But I do believe two things. First, some parents don't know what to do. Second, most parents today are doing what parents of yesterday did: trying to solve their problems at home. Most parents believe that once the school has spoken, it's their responsibility to deal with their child. They may do all the wrong things in the wrong ways — or take positive steps which correct the problem. But the vast majority take some action. You might be surprised to find how often poor grades and notes sent home bring severe reprimands as well as "groundings," withdrawal of privileges, and even physical punishments.

Regardless of what may or may not happen at home, a teacher must communicate and share the responsibility with parents. We can't really expect to help students to the greatest extent possible unless both we and parents are striving for the same objectives. That's why home action should be consistent with school action.

Without teacher communication with parents, our situation is like that of a doctor diagnosing an illness and failing to give medication or instructions for health care. If there's one mistake a professional teacher can never make, it's prejudging whether or not parents care about their children. If there's a worse mistake, it's doing nothing because of that prejudgment. Regardless of what parents do or don't do, our responsibility to relate to and seek assistance from parents does not lessen — and must be a part of our strategic action.

The Real Questions

The real questions for the professional teacher to answer are:

- When to tell parents.
- What and how to tell parents.
- Where to tell parents.

Parents should be told *when* we identify a problem or see anything, positive or negative, which they should know. The communication should not be delayed. However, we must be fully informed before visiting with parents. Consulting with administrators, counselors, and other teachers prior to parent communication is a must. Colleagues can be a tremendous help in identifying the problem and aiding in its solution. Before a parent conference, a teacher should know exactly what the problem is, have specific examples to describe his or her feelings or to relate incidents, and be prepared to give advice for cooperative home and school action. If we don't know what to do, then we should be prepared to recommend specific professional help.

What to tell parents is the truth. That means the truth from both sides of the desk. If there are any unusual aspects, such as personality conflicts, let parents know. Remember, you are sharing a responsibility. Parents can best help if they are dealing with truth.

How you relate information to parents is very important. Be tactful and professional, but don't minimize or exaggerate the situation. Never tell parents that you have lost all hope regarding their child. If you have, then you are the real problem. Remember, you are the professional teacher, and you should give parents the feeling that you are willing to help them and their child.

Sometimes the *where* to talk to parents can be difficult. However, never communicate the details of a problem by letter or telephone. Each of these methods is excellent for arranging a meeting, but the teacher should insist on a personal visit to relate details. This conference should be held in the office of the counselor or administrator or in the teacher's classroom.

Summary

You must operate on the assumption that parents are responsible for their children. Functioning on the basis that parents care about their children and have a right to be involved in anything that involves their child is the best strategic action. Therefore, you must assume that contact will be welcomed by parents. If this assumption concerning parents proves to be wrong, you must increase all efforts to help the child, because your responsibility has doubled.

Never prejudge parents. Lack of time is a poor reason for not contacting parents, because, in truth, a teacher doesn't have time "not to correct" a problem. After all, a class problem is the real consumer of time for both the teacher and other students — as well as for the student who is misbehaving.

If you don't adopt a strategic action which utilizes every resource possible in helping students, you can't fulfill your responsibility as a professional teacher. And parents are a vital resource in gaining good school behavior. If we don't share responsibility with parents, we have moved beyond our authority as classroom teachers. Then, not only are we our own obstacles in helping children solve their problems, but we have also become part of the problem.

PART FIFTEEN

OWNERSHIP IS A KEY TO CHANGING BEHAVIOR

Strategic Action Rationale: Instilling a sense of ownership and sharing power are the most powerful creators of appropriate behavior and self-discipline in a classroom and in a school.

Leon Lessinger, one of the fathers of the A-Bomb, quit his work as a scientist to devote his life to education. He says that there are three things that make people successful. First, they must feel that they're successful. Second, they must feel that others feel they're successful. Third, they must feel a sense of ownership. I couldn't agree more with his beliefs. And teachers need to give students these attributes if they want them to demonstrate appropriate behavior and be successful in school.

In schools, we do a good job regarding the first two success requirements. We don't fare so well on ownership. Maybe we haven't thought about ownership insofar as students are concerned. Or, it might be that we have reservations about giving kids a degree of power and feelings of ownership in classrooms or schools. We shouldn't. When young people develop a sense of ownership toward their school, the benefits to staff and students alike are tremendous. Ownership is a powerful motivator and one of the most significant factors, if not the single most significant factor, in developing self-discipline and demonstrating good citizenship in a school.

A Close Look Will Reveal That Kids Don't "Tear Up" What Belongs To Them

We don't have to look far to see how much people want ownership. There's a company that's sold a lot of insurance by selling people "a piece of the rock." In truth, this is one of the primary reasons behind all movements: women's, labor, black. People wanted a piece of the rock. It's even the basic reason behind Teacher Negotiation Committees. This whole movement resulted, in part, because teachers wanted to feel ownership.

Ownership is a strong motivator because it has a lot to do with a primary human need: security. As teachers, we need to look at how ownership really motivates people in our society — and see how we can adapt it to our classrooms. I know I'm motivated to mow my own lawn, but I'm not necessarily motivated to mow my neighbor's. And I don't see kids tearing up their own cars in the parking lot. They're polishing them. That's because they own them.

We may see kids breaking windows and vandalizing auditoriums, cafeterias, and restrooms. That's because, in their minds, kids *aren't* wrecking *their* school. They're mutilating *our* school. The question is: What can we do to create classrooms and schools where kids feel successful, where they feel others see them as successful, and most importantly, where kids have a sense of responsibility which comes from ownership?

We Must Give Kids Ownership And It Should Be Public Knowledge

In truth, we often say that "schools are for kids." We even proclaim, "It's their school, not ours." Yet, such is not the real practice and we need to recognize that giving kids ownership has a great deal to do with our own security. We must be secure enough to risk student failure before we can give kids any aspect of ownership in a classroom or school. That's because giving kids any ownership means giving them a degree of power.

We can begin giving kids a sense of ownership through class rules and regulations. We can also realize that involvement in what's happening to them in the classroom is vital. Giving students a measure of control over their own lives is the biggest key. When it comes to academics, we can seek student input before and after lessons. We can ask what interested them the most or the least. We can ask them how they would like to tackle a project, and then respond accordingly.

Make no mistake, however. To give students some authority and then try to hide the fact will not give them a sense of ownership. This is exactly what we do when we distribute books or assign lockers, then call them our responsibility. Remember, ownership must be public knowledge to be a motivator. It would be meaningless for us as adults to own a home, for instance, if we could not tell anyone that we did. Therefore, we must talk to students about ownership openly — and make sure they know what we mean. It is a mistake to give them a voice without teaching them that with ownership comes responsibility. When we give students a measure of control over their lives, we should teach them what specific responsibilities they have in each area of ownership.

If we really want students to develop a sense of ownership, it's easy to help them do so. Opportunities to seek input and share responsibility are countless in a classroom. We can let them help establish rules and regulations, involve them in classroom maintenance, and even have advisory groups. A student task force for each of the various projects in our classes, including teacher needs for maintaining an environment necessary for learning, is a healthy idea. And we can extend to faculty the same privileges. It might be wise to have a faculty committee on student and teacher needs and opportunities — as well as a committee for school climate. If you want to teach self-discipline effectively, adopt the strategic action of giving students, including those who are discipline problems, a sense of ownership. And don't be afraid that students will be too lenient in their expectations of others or of themselves. Rather, give guidance or they will be *too hard* on each other as well as themselves.

Summary

We know great things can happen when kids believe it is their school. Students feel responsibility rather than a need to blame. They are positioned to accept responsibility for their own academic condition and behavior. And when they do, the lives of teachers are greatly improved — automatically.

That's why we must give more than lip service to creating a school where kids feel successful, others think they are successful, and they feel ownership. We must adopt a strategic action plan to help kids gain all three — in our classrooms and in the school.

When we do, students will get out of school what we intend them to get. Discipline will improve. There will be fewer crises — and students will get more rewards. And this shouldn't surprise us. After all, schools weren't created to provide an ownership sanctuary for adults. Rather, schools were created to meet students' needs. Indeed, it is their school. If we instill this sense of ownership, we may produce students who do better behaviorally as well as academically in our classes.

PART SIXTEEN

DON'T TALK PAST THE POINT OF BEING INFLUENTIAL

Strategic Action Rationale: Once a point is made and accepted in discipline situations, teacher dominance can negate both gains and influence.

Just as we must know about positive discipline techniques, we need to identify the negative ones as well. A negative that's easy to tag — but not so simple to eliminate — is talking past a point of being influential. It's a topic that needs discussing to refine for both quality and effectiveness in handling misbehavior.

As Teachers, We Know That We Can't Discipline Without Talking, But...

As teachers, we're told we must be dynamic to influence students. And none can deny that we can hardly apply any strategic action through constant silence or practice the art of changing behavior through silence. Yet, we need to recognize that our talking can get in our way. It may be that we're not counseling, but trying to tell or dominate in discipline situations. And when it comes to persuading or correcting a problem student, we may talk past a point of being influential. In truth, kids may turn us off halfway through our lessons or our points.

Once we have captured students' attention and are experiencing the feeling of being influential, it's often a temptation to extend, embellish, or widen every concept. There's nothing wrong with this practice — unless enough has been said already. In truth, teachers who are dynamic and who motivate students do two things. First, they learn to make a point succinctly, and then cease. Second, they learn how to involve students in participating in what they have said.

Once we have made our point and students begin to accept it, we have to be watchful again. As children begin to offer input, we're quite likely to pick up a cue that adds to our original points — and we begin talking again. This can be fatal in terms of kids being cut off and feeling that what they have to say about their own situations really has little or no importance. Students are told over and over that when others are speaking, they are to listen. Unfortunately, adults tend to listen less — without putting boundaries on their allowance. To put it bluntly, we often have a tendency to hog the scene when it comes to talking in discipline situations.

The Evidence Would Indicate That As Kids Grow Capable Of Input, We Cut Them Off

It's more than a passing curiosity that, as people grow older, they're also more able to offer and respond to ideas and teaching. There are many things we can do as teachers to encourage and guarantee student participation in changing behavior — and to make sure we aren't talking too much. Of course, we can plan our counseling so that student participation takes place by design rather than by chance. In addition, we can make certain strategic actions a part of our style. We can know what we're going to say — and know when to quit saying it in an attempt to gain additional acceptance. Equally important, we can stop laboring points after they have been accepted.

We can also refuse to stretch or exaggerate points or to be overzealous when disciplining a student. We can also resolve not to answer questions too quickly. Rather, we can give quick attention and encourage students to find out the answers. Above all, we can let students make their points. When we do, we may find many more kids listening — and responding — in positive rather than silent ways to our efforts to change inappropriate behavior.

Summary

Speaking in influential ways is an art. It's almost like ballet. In a discipline situation, however, it cannot be a solo dance. Content is vital. Timing is essential. Length is of paramount importance. And we must be aware of that magical moment when we can either encourage acceptance or ruin everything. If we continue unaware, our dance may go on, but we shall dance alone.

Talking influentially is really a matter of balance. That balance is among talking, listening, participating, and allowing students to participate. Knowing when to speak and when not to speak is an integral part of the art of developing your strategic action in discipline situations. When you have made a point, quit. And when you quit, let students begin thinking very seriously about what has been said. It's at this point that participation and meaningful learning begin for a student regarding his or her behavior. That's why these techniques should be a part of your strategic action when correcting, counseling, and reprimanding students.

PART SEVENTEEN

SEED PLANTING

Strategic Action Rationale: Short statements of shared objective truths can be more powerful motivators than long conversations in getting students to change their behavior. Likewise, short statements of objective truth are excellent tools to prepare students for private conferences.

As previously discussed, refraining from talking too much when disciplining students is not an easy thing to do. That's why when a child clings to an attitude or behavior that is disruptive or self-defeating, a teacher needs a special technique to arouse human change. As we have said — and as every teacher has experienced — long conversations of guidance, regardless of their sincerity, often prove fruitless. The teacher talks, the student listens, and the stalemate remains. This situation has frustrated teachers and parents alike for centuries.

When teachers find themselves in these situations, they should abandon normal persuasive techniques and begin planting seeds. Seed planting is offering or responding with a *short comment of objective truth* — without further conversation. Often a word, an opinion, or a simple statement of fact given without elaboration over a period of time can do more to help change a student's attitude or behavior than any other action. This is especially true if that student attitude or behavior and yours are in total conflict.

But there are some conditions a teacher must remember when planting seeds. One can't impose one's truth on another — one can only offer it out of one's self. Truth is not textbook oriented, and a teacher's humbleness must precede the offering. Superiority must never be felt or revealed by its giver. Rather, a child must feel that by age and experience alone, the teacher has naturally experienced some realities that students have not. This is the teacher's truth — but it may not necessarily be an acceptable truth to a child. The best a teacher can do is share his or her truth with a child. It cannot be forced. No truth can be seeded this way. Therefore, the art of seed planting is not an easy art for a teacher to put into his or her repertoire of strategic action skills. Yet, it is one of the most effective of all motivators in getting kids to change their behavior and adopt new attitudes.

Helping Children Change

A teacher should not develop this art for student manipulation — and there is a difference between assistance and manipulation. The difference lies in the area of professional intent. However, there are many instances when a teacher knows a truth, yet cannot get a child to do what would be best for him or her because the teacher's idea, opinion, or belief is in total opposition to that which is held by the child. Failure to help a student help himself or herself causes teacher frustration. Worse, after repeated failure to persuade a student, a teacher may quit trying to help.

Examples in a school are countless for students and staff alike. For instance, often a child will not participate in class. Or, despite continuous urging, a talented child will not play an instrument or participate in athletics. Likewise, several conferences may fail to change a student's mind about being tardy, skipping school, or dropping out of school because he or she hates class or even a teacher. These and certain other situations have produced, it seems to us, student attitudes that seem beyond change. In reality, they may indeed remain fixed — if they are confronted in the usual way.

The usual way to try to influence a student's behavior or attitude is to think in terms of a private talk or conference where you and the student can talk things out. We may even get groups of educators, parents, and the child to each conference. It is normal to think that when we explain all the facts and benefits of changing the student's opinions of school, of classmates, of studying hard, of behaving, the student will change his or her attitude. It is normal to expect an immediate, final solution to the problems after such a meeting. We might even be willing to have two, three, or four such talks or conferences before a change in attitude or behavior results. However, after the fourth talk — when we are still receiving the same total opposition — frustration is likely to replace understanding. In fact, we might even "throw in the towel" and quit trying to help this student.

A Time For Seeds...Not Trees

An attitude change, whether in a student or in a colleague, is best approached by planting a seed rather than attempting to tear a tree from its roots and then transplant it in alien soil. The kernel of this seed is simple, honest, and objective truth. When you learn to be a seed planter, patience becomes your asset. Professional truth becomes your partner. Being a seed planter involves making only a short statement followed by a simple assertion of belief, without any connotation or hint of judgment. It requires the elimination of any lengthy conversations until you believe the seed is beginning to grow. For instance, a teacher can tell a potential dropout four or five things in as many conversations to plant seeds when the student speaks about quitting school. You'll be amazed by the thought evoked in a student contemplating quitting school when a teacher says simply:

- I don't know ... I enjoy my freedom too much.
- Dropping out is fine, if you could always get the job you wanted.
- I would never put myself in a position where someone else could control my life.
- I don't know ... I want to be happy when I'm thirty.
- I don't know ... I want all the chances I can get.
- I wouldn't want to tell my kids that I quit.

Even though an offered seed may be openly opposed and rejected — it has been planted — and the student cannot get it out of his or her head. The more he or she tries, the deeper the roots will grow. Once planted, the seed of objective truth is there and a student must deal with it privately and personally. His or her mind may harbor opposition, but a mind will not permit rejection if the seed contains truth and self-interest.

If a student begins to accept the truth of an idea, then talking with the student about further truths becomes easier. Few human minds can prevent a truth from growing, even if they externally reject it. Truth has a way of growing once it is planted. That's why seed planting is a very powerful strategic action.

Summary

Sometimes children accept guidance better when teachers forget about long conversations and begin by planting the seeds of honest and objective truth. These seeds must also be continually nourished by teacher understanding and sincerity, if they are to germinate and grow.

When a truthful insight does surface, it has been there all the time. A student has only persisted in burying it within until someone or something helped it to emerge. Often we hear teachers say, "Jimmy has finally seen the light," or "Jane has really come into her own." What they really mean is that a healthy attitude has finally emerged. It was only buried. Now it has surfaced. It was there all the time. When seed planting rather than harassment is your strategic action, you'll find more students discovering their own light.

PART EIGHTEEN

THREE DAMAGING ACTIONS: THE PUT-DOWN, THE PUT-ON, AND THE PUT-OFF

Strategic Action Rationale: The put-down, put-on, and put-off are three completely different behaviors used as self-servers. But they usually cause those who use them to fail.

The put-down, put-on, and put-off are commonly used. But they are more than behaviors revealed by teachers and students. They are techniques people use against other people. Unfortunately, they can become habits. They are easy traps, for the risk of falling into them exists daily in a school.

One reason it's easy to fall into the habit of using the put-down, put-on, and put-off is that we think they work. In fact, using them may make us feel superior, smart, or clever. We may even think others regard us the same way. Yet, close observation will reveal that these three techniques only allow those who use them to fool themselves momentarily. They are three bad habits that hold us back from success. We need to break them. To do so, we need to understand each of these actions. Each is different, and if we want to develop effective strategic actions we must know each one, and eliminate it from our actions in discipline situations.

Analyzing The Put-Down

The put-down always has to do with victimizing students. It is used most often to show superiority. We employ it to ward off something that surprises or perplexes us, or makes us angry. Most often the use of the put-down is spontaneous. For a teacher, it's a personal reaction in a professional situation. Some teachers habitually and automatically use the put-down in discipline situations. One thing is certain: It is used when a teacher does not know the right thing to do. By using it, one can pretend superiority when inferiority is the real feeling.

The put-down in teaching is revealed through the use of sarcasm and any other words that degrade. Unfortunately, the put-down always says to students that we don't approve of or like them. It is an open show of disrespect in the most uncaring and inconsiderate way. This action violates every teaching rule and has no place in our schools. That's why we need to remind ourselves, continually, not to use the put-down. To demean any individual for any reason should be beneath our dignity and intellect. This habit can be broken. We need only remind ourselves to say nothing unless we have something of value and relevance to offer — regardless of the situation. Then, we need to take action which builds rather than destroys.

The Put-On

The put-on has to do with ourselves more than students. It allows us to pretend we know something we don't or to be someone we aren't — momentarily. However, it's another technique which gives us the opposite of what we want as professional teachers. Usually, the put-on is used as a ploy to raise our image in the eyes of others. Unfortunately, though it may make us feel more important for the moment, it does not make others feel we are important.

The put-on is used in many ways. We pretend knowledge or pretend that we are doing something important when we're not. We pretend we're interested in what a student is saying when we're not, and our nonverbal language indicates otherwise. We indicate patronizing agreement when disagreement is our tone. That's the key to the put-on. It has, in one way or another, an air of phoniness. This is one of the reasons it never works. It is never genuine. We need to remind ourselves of one fact to gain the motivation needed to break this habit and eliminate it from our repertoire of discipline techniques forever: Students see through it immediately. Students cannot and will not relate to its use or to the teacher who uses it.

The Put-Off

The put-off always has to do with getting out of something. Most of us have been guilty of using the put-off. Sometimes we use it simply to gain more time. Yet, it is often used to avoid doing a task or handling a problem. It is also used to avoid submitting to failure. Sometimes it is used to pretend we are on top of something when we are not.

The put-off can get the most conscientious teachers into trouble. It can cause us to delay action. It can also cause us to make promises to students that we can't or don't intend to keep. I asked a young student recently when his class was going on its field trip, and he disappointedly replied, "The teacher said we aren't going." Surprised, I asked, "What did your teacher say?" To this, the youngster replied, "He said *maybe* we would go — but his maybe always means no."

The put-off can also allow us to pass the buck to someone else. This put-off may hurt our positions with students. We can't talk to students about meeting their responsibilities when we don't meet ours. That's a fact. Mostly, though, the put-off makes students doubt our sincerity and integrity — and for good reason.

Summary

The put-down, put-on, and put-off are bad habits people fall into for any of several reasons. They usually give us the opposite of what we want as teachers. They make us look ignorant when we want to appear intelligent. They make us look untruthful rather than truthful, unprofessional rather than professional. Worse, they drive students away from us rather than toward us.

In all of our various methods, techniques, and behaviors, we need to examine three things. We need to look at how we feel about students. We also need to know how we treat students as a result of our feelings. Finally, we need to know what kinds of behavior we project to students when we are trying to protect our images and positions as teachers. Our answers should help get the direction of our strategic action in every discipline situation on proper course.

Students are turned off by phoniness no matter what its form. They will come to dislike anything and anyone who demeans their intelligence in any way. The put-down, put-on, and put-off are phony as well as demeaning. That's why we must fight falling into these traps. The put-down, put-on, and put-off may be easy traps to fall into. And without the strategic action which totally eliminates them from teacher behavior, these traps cannot be avoided.

PART NINETEEN

THREE ROADBLOCKS IN DISCIPLINE: ALIBIS, OBJECTIONS, AND COMPLAINTS

Strategic Action Rationale: Alibis, objections, and complaints are three separate behaviors with three different motivations. Unless they are handled separately, failure rather than success becomes the probability in discipline situations.

If we haven't heard every student alibi, objection, and complaint after a single year of teaching, we most certainly will. They cause us to be angry — and they are roadblocks to effective teaching. But these three student behaviors have differences. We need to recognize this fact before we can handle them successfully. And we need to recognize that these are three different behaviors. They can't be lumped together and treated the same way.

Alibis, objections, and complaints can't be ignored if we want to cut their frequency. That's why our first rule must be to listen. The majority of these teaching obstacles will dissolve if we do. Many will disappear if we just say, "What shall *we* do?" rather than react angrily or defensively. Let's talk about how to deal professionally with these three common occurrences, especially in children who are discipline problems.

Student Alibis

Alibis are quite different from objections and complaints. If they are not treated differently, big problems can result. It's easy to see why. Mainly, students offering alibis *have lost interest* in the activity related to the alibi. A teacher must remember this fact when handling these students.

The alibi is expressed by such token offerings as, "I was too busy," or "I'm going to do it tomorrow," or "My mother lost my notes." A teacher must attempt to analyze the *cause* of the alibi — not the alibi itself. Can the student do the work? Is the assignment missing something in the eyes of the student? Would the student do something else better? If so, we might be much better off altering or changing the assignment rather than holding to a dead-end course. Remember, lack of interest is the primary reason behind most alibis.

Until we discover the reason behind the alibi, here are some strategic actions we can employ to get the behavior we need. Listen closely and respond fast. If a student says, "I lost my pencil," we should say, "Here's another." If a student says, "I can't find my book," we can reply, "Here's a loaner." If a student offers the alibi, "I lost my paper," respond quickly, "You can have more time." Then, ask to see the student later to find the real cause behind the alibi. When we do this, we are positioned to deal with the real problem.

Student Objections

Student objections usually contain the word *but.* They are expressed by such phrases as, "But ... I don't know how to do it," or "But ... you didn't say I had to do it today," or "But ... I didn't have time."

In reality, the response is caused by a student wanting or expecting more — whether it's more teacher help, more information, or an extended date for turning in an assignment. Of paramount importance, objecting students *may* still have an interest in class work. This is vitally important to the teacher handling the objection. That's why teacher analysis of the reason for the objection is important. We need to ask ourselves four questions which will guide our approach with the objecting student.

- Is the objection intelligent?
- Is ignorance revealed by the objection?
- Is the objection emotional?
- Is the objection analytical?

We should listen to every objection. If the objection has merit, share points of agreement. But the benefits of our rationale must outweigh the student objection or the objection cannot be overcome. If the student is wrong, we must educate and let the student down gracefully. This is a must. In either case, ask questions rather than tell, give benefits rather than ultimatums, and relate assurances rather than demands. Using these three strategic actions will give us more success in handling objections.

Student Complaints

Student complaints are usually the result of some kind of upset. They are expressed by saying, "This isn't fair," and "I don't think we should have to do this." There's one important facet of complaints a teacher can't overlook: Inherent in complaints is interest. Furthermore, complaints usually contain involvement. That's why if we ignore a complaining student, we may turn interest off.

Complaints require a full explanation. For best results, allow a student to say what is on his or her mind. If the student is totally or partially right, correct the situation immediately and thank the student for bringing the complaint to your attention. If the student is wrong, explain and give assurance in a caring way. Above all, don't do anything that makes either the student or the complaint appear unimportant. Remember, once you turn off interest, you turn off motivation automatically. Then, apathy becomes the problem and this is much more difficult to handle than *any* complaint.

Summary

Alibis, objections, and complaints are inherent in teaching — and in discipline situations. All are different in nature and need to be approached and managed differently. If we lump them together and try to treat all in the same way, our chances for failure are greater than our chances for success.

All three of these student behaviors require listening. However, each must be handled differently after this beginning point. We either respond professionally to alibis, objections, and complaints, or we do not. If we respond in less than a professional way, we will not correct the situation. Worse, our response can affect every student in our class. It's when students say we don't and won't listen that many of our other problems begin.

In truth, all our teaching skills and discipline techniques are of no avail unless we are positioned to teach. That's why we must handle alibis, objections, and complaints skillfully. If we don't, then we may find ourselves offering one of these three roadblocks as the reason why we can't be effective in the classroom. That's why we must make accepting rather than refusing part of our strategic action when it comes to alibis, objections, and complaints.

PART TWENTY

SYMPATHY AND EMPATHY

Strategic Action Rationale: If the difference between sympathy and empathy is not understood, teacher actions may actually promote the behavior we are trying to discourage.

There are two important realities that we must all recognize in order to change inappropriate behavior to appropriate behavior. First, every teacher is a counselor. Second, the classroom teacher is best positioned to counsel students who are not behaving appropriately. That's why it's very important that we understand the words sympathy and empathy. Such understanding may alter our strategic action approach and technique and make us more effective when counseling young people. Discussing the difference between sympathy and empathy is not very difficult in terms of definition. The problem comes in application.

Likewise, sometimes we get the impression that one of the two is "good" and the other "bad." This isn't so. There are times when we must be sympathetic and other times when we need to be empathetic. It isn't that we must never be either one, or that we must always be both. It's important, however, to discern what the differences are. Most important, our strategic action must *not deny* these two teacher offerings to students because they are misbehaving.

A Definite Place

Being sympathetic is completely in order when a tragedy befalls someone. It's important to feel sorry and even to mourn. By being sympathetic, we encourage and promote ventilation of feelings. Sympathy under such conditions is a supportive and loving gesture to offer. Make no mistake, it is completely positive under such circumstances. By validating how the other person is feeling, we encourage strength through tears. This is a healthy kind of sympathy.

On the other hand, if we have a depressed student who deals in gloom from morning until night, we add to the debilitation by giving only sympathy. Karen Horney, the noted psychoanalyst, said some years back that one does not cure a neurosis with kindness. In such circumstances, sympathy merely promotes further depression because it doesn't offer anything substantial that the other person can get a handle on. This is an unhealthy kind of sympathy. Yet, this is exactly what we may do once we lower our expectations or expect a child to behave badly.

Empathy is an art. It's the ability to put ourselves in the position of someone else. Through empathy, we really can feel and understand another's pain or joy. In the case of pain, we can say some positive things that might be of help — and we need to say them. Remember, self-pitying students are depressed. We promote this state by being sympathetic. Sometimes, in fact, abrasiveness — without cruelty — may be much more helpful than agreement about how awful life is.

When I say empathy is an art, I mean that there is a delicate balance between empathy and sympathy at times. It takes a very sensitive teacher to know the difference and act on it. Some teachers confuse the attitude involved in empathy with removing feelings altogether. This isn't how it should be. We can feel intense concern and sympathy for someone, and at the same time know that expressing only that feeling will not mitigate the suffering but, perhaps, increase it. If we are really tuned in to that person, we will approach with *concerned empathy.* However, we will encourage positive action on the part of that student as well. This stance must, therefore, be a part of our strategic action.

When Dealing With Students

When dealing with our students, we must balance our sympathy and empathy very carefully. We should always move toward the positive approach, for children grow more through the positive than through the negative — especially when they are being disciplined. True, students may learn from the negative, but they are much more likely to grow, and change both attitude and behavior, through the positive. As teachers, we must never forget this fact. Too often, we make a misbehaving child learn too much from negatives because the positives are so few. We do the same when dealing with parents, too. When there is a problem with a child, parents often become defensive. We need to tell them that we understand their reaction

— but that such an approach won't help solve the problem. By saying this to parents, we have stated our sympathy and have moved on into empathy. It's in empathy, not in sympathy, that we will find a solution. That's why we need to move more often in this direction than in any other.

We truly put our performance and competency on the line when we are called on to make the choice between these two strategic action approaches in dealing with problem students. We have to depend on our know-how, experience, and genuine caring to get us through. They will — if we keep in mind that we can give sympathy as a first comment, but that we must often move into empathy if we are interested in progress or a shift in behavior on the part of the student. If we don't, we may not be helping students to solve their problems. Rather, we may be helping to perpetuate them without meaning to, and it's all because we don't understand the difference between sympathy and empathy.

Summary

We often find that the misbehaving child and the self-pitying child are the unmotivated ones. That's because these students spend all their time excusing themselves from everything. We can, through our empathy, help them to evaluate where they are and, perhaps, even why they have arrived at this point. We can't do this with sympathy alone.

Through teaching, children can come to understand that they have choices all along the way. And these choices are theirs, not ours. However, some choices belong to us as well. We need to tell students that they can either do nothing and vegetate, or choose the positive road and move. We can help them come to this point, not through sympathy, but through empathy. When we help students to arrive at such conclusions, they are likely to improve behaviorally as well as academically, which means their whole view of living and learning in school will change.

Teachers have many professional commitments and obligations. One of the biggest is to know the difference between sympathy and empathy. Both are tools that enable us to do our jobs better and become better people in the process. And this, after all, is one of our primary objectives. That's why our professional strategic action should employ both sympathy and empathy.

PART TWENTY-ONE

BENEFIT OF THE DOUBT

Strategic Action Rationale: If student guarantees must precede teacher trust, not only is a teacher destined for disappointment, but students will also be frequently victimized by teacher prejudgment. In addition, unfairness will be the tone of the classroom, and the risking necessary to teach self-discipline will not exist.

- I'll believe it when I see it ...
- You'll have to show me ...
- Let's see if you can do it first ...

There seems to be something in the nature of people that says, "prove it." Maybe that's one of the reasons it's so difficult to give students the benefit of the doubt. We seem to feel better — and even more secure — if we can avoid any risk taking and make people prove themselves out of our doubts rather than our trust. We need to be aware of this possibility, or our doubts can come between us and those we teach — permanently.

Out Of Our Nature

Is there one of us who has not agonized over whether to give a borderline student a C or a B? The reality is that we can often build a better case for the C. There's no doubt that other factors such as student attitude and effort are included in our consideration. However, the biggest consideration should be whether the student will be better off being encouraged by the higher grade or discouraged by the lower one. This is the real issue. Here, our human nature may work against acting in students' best interest.

Many teachers would give the lower grade because they believe people are strengthened by the blows they receive. The whole Western world has functioned on such beliefs for some time. Thus the name "Victorian" was given. Much can be said in favor of the virtue of hard work, but if it begins to border on hard-line obsessiveness, then we had better question its validity. If we can never receive the benefit of the doubt — or give it ourselves — a constant struggle against overwhelming odds is the emblem under which we live. It will rule our every belief and govern our every action, especially in discipline situations. A misbehaving student may have to prove himself or herself for a long time before he or she receives the benefit of the doubt from us. And it's unlikely that many kids will keep trying to prove themselves to us. Rather, they will quit trying. That's why giving the benefit of the doubt must be a part of our strategic action. If it isn't, many students will revert to old patterns rather than try to give us guarantees, function under our cloud, and prove themselves to us continually.

This is not to say that there are not those times when the lower grade ought to be given or trust withheld. Most certainly, there will be many such times. However, such actions should not be taken every time for the same subjective reasons. In cases when we don't know what to do after careful consideration, it might be best to choose a positive course which offers at least a chance of constructive outcomes. It might be wise to opt for the higher grade or special privileges and include a personal talk with the student regarding our decision. How much better it is in human terms to explain why we are choosing to trust that they will do better next time — than to choose the lower grade or denial and say we hope the student will prove himself or herself worthy in the future. How much more encouraging it is to be willing to err or risk being wrong on the positive side than to come down heavily on the negative side.

Risking Uncertainty

We need to be willing to risk in moments of uncertainty. No matter what we might think, we stand to lose very little. We might be wise to remember this fact with the student who has disappointed us in the past. Maybe we can, if we realize the student probably was more disappointed in himself or herself than we were. A teacher simply cannot afford to label a child forever because of past experiences. If we are so sure how a student will respond to our considerations — and we refuse him or her the benefit of the doubt — we make all decisions on the basis of past behavior and allow no room for change in the present. This is a mistake and is unfair. Looking back on our own lives should prove this fact.

Not a single one of us has a background void of mistakes. Would we be happy to be judged negatively, and allowed a minimum of trust, as a result of those moments of bad judgment? This is what happens to children frequently.

I remember an eighth-grade student who returned from a boys' reformatory at midterm with a record of hostility and hatred toward authority. He came into the room heavy with bad attitudes. The teacher made a point of welcoming him to the class. He looked surprised — but spent the hour nonverbally registering his learned disinterest. After class, the teacher said it was probably tough transferring under the circumstances, but that she sensed from his record that his ability to perform was good. She reminded him that this was a new beginning — and asked whether he would be willing to read and discuss a passage for the class the next day. He said, "I don't think so." She said it was all right, and that they would wait until class for his decision. The next day she asked him again to read, and after only a brief hesitation, he did. She had given this student the benefit of a large doubt. It paid off in a new beginning. Without such trust and risk, nothing would have changed. That's the difference between a professional teacher and one who is not — and this particular teacher made the benefit of the doubt a vital part of her strategic action.

Summary

Opportunities to give students the benefit of the doubt arise daily. These opportunities are as good for us as they are for students. After all, ours is a profession which deals constantly with growth. Change is as inherent in growth as it is in opportunity. Ours is also a profession which deals with failure as well as with potentials and possibilities. If we lock ourselves into refusing to give students the benefit of the doubt, we lock ourselves into a future based only on past failures. We place ourselves in a position where nothing can happen for students until they prove something to us. Unfortunately, this is one of the reasons many misbehaviors continue. We talk, we reprimand, we counsel — but we refuse to risk.

When we can allow the benefit of the doubt, we can become the agents of change rather than only its recorders. When we can move past our reluctance to give students the benefit of the doubt, we have moved to the point at which we can accept our students as they are. Being able to grant such allowances can make us feel a true sense of progress for ourselves as well as those we teach. That's when the stage is set for learning, and especially for changing behavior. These are the reasons that adopting strategic actions which include risk and giving students the benefit of the doubt can help us change inappropriate behavior to appropriate behavior. Adopting such a stance can also add fun, excitement, and hope to the process.

PART TWENTY-TWO

CHANGING STUDENT HABITS

Strategic Action Rationale: Enforcement of good habits and providing alternatives to detrimental habits are necessities in teaching self-discipline as well as in achieving appropriate behavior in the classroom.

In many ways humans are enigmas. So often we crave and seek out that which hurts us. So it is with the development of some behavioral habits. Habits are those practices we routinely repeat until they become unconscious, almost compulsive, parts of our behavior. We see all kinds of habits appear at different stages of our development. Some stay with us for a lifetime. Some can be more easily shed than others — as the smoker soon finds out when he or she tries to quit.

There are personal physical habits, work habits, attitudinal habits, and habits necessary for good health and safety. Children brush their teeth. Mothers grab their children's hands when crossing a street. Men carry their wallets in the same pocket. The grouchy boss "barks" at his or her employees. In wars, even killing becomes a habit.

When people are forced to change their habits, they often rebel. Habits are routinely comfortable. Too, habits reduce the necessity of instigating the complex processes of decision making. People don't have to think "why" they do or do not do something — they just do it because that's the way they have always done it. There's security in this kind of behavior — and this is a laziness that makes life a little more comfortable. That's why habits can become a way of life.

Reinforcement...

Teachers are faced daily with teaching "habitized" youngsters. We should never lose sight of this reality. Many of the habits students have developed by age six or sixteen are just as deeply entrenched as those the teacher may have acquired in twice as many years. And like everyone else, the student will have difficulty changing habits. Many students don't even want to change them.

Recognizing and understanding the process of habit development, we can see that teachers have essentially three functions: to reinforce good habits, and to use the self-preservation and substitute techniques. First, they must *reinforce and strengthen* those habits which are good for a student, those which the student needs to pursue during his or her present stage of development or maybe even for a lifetime. Too many teachers harp on bad student habits and ignore good ones. This is a strategic action mistake. Certainly, not all habits are bad. Those students who have developed a habit of politeness need to be encouraged to continue it. The second grader who hangs up his or her coat without being told to needs approval for this behavior. The high school senior who comes in for extra help should be given reinforcement for this course of action rather than scolded for coming for help so late. These good habits cannot be ignored or turned into negatives. They must be reinforced in positive ways if they are to remain a part of the student's behavior pattern.

Most important though, while reinforcing habits, teachers must remember to help students learn that they should never let their habits consume them. Care should be taken, even with some good habits, not to allow them to become "sacred." Without doubt, "sacred" habits can impede progress, stifle creativity, and hinder personal happiness and fulfillment. They are often the cause of missed opportunities and a dull, monotonous life. As teachers, we need to remember this fact too.

...And Alternatives

There are those habits, though, which need to be eradicated. For obvious reasons, a student would simply be better off if a certain behavioral pattern were erased. There can be many reasons a habit needs to be changed. It may be to help a student become socially acceptable or to help him or her in both private and professional life. Whatever the reason, though, the student will generally resist change — whether it be from tardiness, lying, smoking, or a negative attitude toward classmates.

Many people, though not all, can be motivated to change a habit for self-preservation. If they realize a habit is self-destructive, they can be motivated to change habitual behaviors which are protective devices in the first place. This *self-preservation technique,* however, is often overused. Teachers must make sure they are not exaggerating when using the self-preservation technique. Remember, only objective and whole truths will make people change habits. Half-truths make students cling to what they are doing.

However, nagging or simply telling a child he or she needs to change an attitude does little good. Often, even giving reasons has little effect on changing behavior. Remember, people almost always insist on hanging on to habits. That's normal. Experience as a teacher should tell you something about that. That's why the *substitute technique* is one of the best strategic action motivators a teacher can use. When a student gives up one habit, he or she needs something to take its place — something to fill the void. The best technique a teacher can employ here is the offering of an alternative behavior pattern to be developed into a beneficial habit. So often a student doesn't know — consciously or subconsciously — that an alternative is needed or what to substitute for a present attitude or behavior. The student has been told over and over that he or she needs to change a bad habit, but no one has taken the time to offer positive steps that he or she can try. Nobody has taken the time to suggest a substitute. Teachers can change student habits when they develop the ability to offer alternative courses of action.

Also, a teacher must never forget that time is required to change a habit and, during this time, continuous improvement is the only reasonable goal. The teacher who expects the student to effect an immediate change has lost sight of the intensity of feelings as well as the force habits have on the lives of all people. Often, the teacher will have to repeat suggestion after suggestion and have several conversations before any visible sign of a habit change occurs.

Summary

We, as professional educators, must remember not to let the bad habits of students consume us — or them. We cannot let student habits frustrate us to the point that we change our behavior toward those we teach because we cannot effect change in their behavior. Nothing could be worse than that — for the student or the teacher.

When we do become frustrated, we close all doors of communication. Experience has taught all of us that this is a truth. Then, a receptivity for new ways of doing things will not be present and we, as teachers, cannot be agents of behavior change. Rather, we remove ourselves from the function of teacher to that of a reinforcer of bad habits.

PART TWENTY-THREE

WHEN GUILT HAS BEEN ESTABLISHED

Strategic Action Rationale: Students who are habitual discipline problems are more familiar with and equipped to counter teacher toughness than they are to handle

gentleness — and will respond positively to compassion in adverse situations.

Needless to say, when we talk to students who are in trouble with us, our upset regarding a situation may cause us to make some mistakes. This is especially true after guilt has been admitted and established as a fact. That's why we can always use strategic action guidelines which become positive and professional conditioned responses in ugly situations. After all, our task is to resolve and defuse a situation rather than to charge it. But with guidelines, we may be able to do both. And we'll feel much better about ourselves in the process — and so will students.

Being Gentle Rather Than Tough Has Professional Advantages For You

First, before you say one word or take any action, honestly explore your attitudes and desires concerning the problem and the child. Examine both — before you even talk with a student. Then, make sure the student realizes that you have examined all the facts and extenuating circumstances — and that your objective is not merely to scold or issue a punishment. Rather, it's to achieve improved behavior. Remember, it's paramount that students feel you are not prejudging them or the situation. In addition, you also want them to know that they have some options — because people don't usually function well with absolutes in personal problem situations. Absolutes leave them without flexibility. This reality is compounded for the student who is a habitual discipline problem.

Second, when you really want to get tough, get gentle. You can't imagine how disarming and effective this strategic action can be. Also realize that a private reprimand is far more effective than one that takes place in front of peers. If you realize that the punishment — even if deserved — won't be nearly as effective as the technique, you should be able to forget being tough on every occasion. It's to your advantage if you do. Likewise, becoming gentle can prepare you to follow a professional course rather than react in personal ways.

Be open, calm, and consistent. Don't demand a complete confession when guilt has already been established. You may ask for an apology, but don't force one, or you may create another problem. Resist being the superior power or creating a win-lose situation. Also, guard against exaggerating about the student's bad behavior. Too, allow yourself — and the student — to be honest in describing events, and expressing values, feelings, and preferences regarding what has happened as well as what will happen as a result of the problem.

Problem Behavior Should Be A Shared Responsibility

Once guilt has been established and students are aware of the fact, it's vitally important to acknowledge openly to them that they can't control all of the situations in which they find themselves. Too, understand that this reality is one reason that a teacher must be a good listener — even when he or she doesn't agree. Only *after* you have listened can you express disappointment. Without this strategic action, the situation is one-sided as far as students are concerned — and they may respond accordingly. They may listen and take their medicine, but they won't change their attitudes or behavior. You can count on this fact of life. Therefore, always tell students you want to hear what they have to say. Never, under any circumstances, say, "I don't want to hear it," or "I'll do the talking; you do the listening" — even after guilt is established — if you want to change attitude or behavior.

Never forget to keep to the issue at hand and the points you're trying to make. Do not use an "all is wrong" approach. The shotgun action will never be accepted by students, including those who are in trouble or those who have confessed to misbehavior. That's why you must keep to the issue and continually emphasize your concern for the student. In a caring way, discuss the real or possible consequences of his or her behavior. In the same breath, discuss some alternatives available to the student. Remember, your purpose is to teach acceptable behavior. Students will not learn it by osmosis. It takes specific teaching, not generalizations. This is a point we often miss. Worse, we often think kids learn proper behavior via the punishment they have received. They do not.

Stay off the soapbox at all times. It is a poor strategic action. If there's any doubt about a portion of guilt in a specific incident, say so. Likewise, if a fact is contested after admission of guilt, you might be wise to drop that particular point. Remember, you can't become angry or vindictive toward students. If you do, you will push the consequences of their misbehavior out of proportion. You can't put these students down publicly, grade them harder, or adopt the attitude that you'll let their behavior hang them either. All are strategic action mistakes which will only worsen a bad situation.

Summary

We are well aware that students in trouble need to be talked with, not at. The purpose of talking is to rebuild, not to further tear down. That's why, when we feel the need to get tough, we ought to consider getting gentle. It is an overwhelmingly successful strategic action.

Remember, any conversation without compassion can destroy love. And if we want compassion, we must give it. In any adverse situation, most students can respond to gentleness. In fact, it can be the best disarmament. Students are seldom critical of teachers who are caring. They seldom challenge teachers' gentleness. In truth, it's our toughness they fight. In addition, know that kids may know more about how to hate and get tough than you do because it's the only response they experience with adults. That's why being gentle can be disarming and render them pliable.

We know we must do more than tell when we are counseling students in trouble with us. We must also show the way. That is, after all, what teaching and counseling for appropriate behavior are all about. And when we teach, we must recognize that a private discussion can become our greatest asset in relating to students and helping them change. It shows our concern. Public reprimand may only indicate we're trying to show power or save face in front of our class. Then, the stage is set for conflicts rather than solutions.

PART TWENTY-FOUR

TAKING KIDS OFF THE HOOK

Strategic Action Rationale: Only one person can initiate and finalize action which brings negative situations to a new beginning in the classroom. That person is the teacher.

It's not uncommon for students who misbehave to get "behind the eight ball" with teachers. A negative attitude, inappropriate behavior, or something said or done in our presence can put students in difficulty with us — and they know it. But children might not know what to do about their predicament. Although what students do about the situations they create is often the issue, it shouldn't be. The real issue is what we decide to do. That's because, in reality, there's only one person in the classroom who can initiate action that can change the situation. And that person is the teacher. That's why adopting a strategic action which includes taking children off the hook, rather than keeping them there, can be so important in discipline situations.

If We Don't Take Kids Off The Hook...

When kids get in trouble with you, what do you do? Do you take them off the hook — or do you let them dangle? After all, when students are in trouble, they often get careful and cautious when we let them dangle. The likelihood of something else happening seems to be reduced. So there's a degree of teacher power — and control — in keeping kids on the hook. Therefore, it might seem as if all the advantages remain in our hands as long as we let students continue to feel that they're in trouble. The minute we relieve the pressure, it may seem as if all our leverage will be lost. That's why many teachers hold to a strategic action of keeping kids uncertain regarding their status in the classroom. This stance can be a big mistake.

A teacher will do well to understand what usually happens in such situations. Often, students' first move is to make repairs. However, a close look will reveal that these efforts can be clumsy — and frequently worse than the act that got them into trouble. For instance, the class clown may get in trouble because of his or her humor, then try to use that humor to ease tensions with the teacher. Therefore, students who are behind the eight ball often compound their problems with more inappropriate behavior of some kind — and there's a reason.

When children are in trouble with adults, they're often unable to act in mature, positive, and corrective ways. It doesn't take an experienced teacher long to realize that these young people usually get depressed, act in negative ways, become apathetic, or grasp for any saving line — and often it's the wrong one. If we can throw in a life line rather than leave the student to struggle, the whole situation can be corrected rather than compounded. We need to ponder this reality. And when we do, we should realize that there's absolutely nothing that we do which does not alter, for better or for worse, the climate of the classroom. As classroom leaders, we have the final responsibility to see that there is leadership. And when a student needs rescuing, we must rescue. That's why adopting a "make things right" strategic action is an absolute necessity.

None Of Us Is Free Of The Need To Be Taken Off The Hook Occasionally

There are some dos and don'ts for handling these discipline situations and teaching students lessons in the process. Unless we follow such guides, we may make every bad situation worse. For instance, we don't want to rush in and tell students they're rotten people. This move only guarantees further deterioration of the situation, lowers self-esteem, and damages the student-teacher relationship. Likewise, we need to allow that students aren't feeling very good about what they said or did either. That's why it's wise to approach students in an easy way by saying, "I'm not comfortable with what's happened. How do you feel about it?"

When we take this strategic action course, no one has been accused or is accusing. We're simply saying how we feel and are inviting students to air their feelings — and maybe their apologies. It might seem as if this course is too simple. It's not. Such a strategic action approach is used over and over by successful teachers who care and who understand the dynamics of human behavior.

None of us is free from the need to be taken off the hook occasionally. We have all felt bad about ourselves for something that we said or did. It's only sad that we don't have friends who understand our need often enough. As professionals, let's not compound these ills by failing to offer such understanding to those we teach.

Summary

Letting kids off the hook may not be acceptable to some teachers. They may think it's coddling. Some may think students should pay heavily for inappropriate behavior. Yet, we know this is true only if we haven't left our Victorian heritage behind and moved out of the frigid, rigid claims that were made on the souls of people. In the past, people who dared to make mistakes were believed unworthy of rescue. If we have learned anything about the whys and hows of human behavior, then we've learned to set aside our first impulse to punish. Instead, we have substituted a need to act firmly but compassionately. That's why we should never meet students' acts of bad behavior with acts of thoughtlessness. When we do, it may be that we are the ones who should be punished if punishment is the issue.

We know human beings respond much more quickly to caring than to rigid punishment. When we take kids off the hook, we at least have a chance to make things better. As long as we leave them on the hook, the situation will usually deteriorate. That's because we are automatically telling kids they're no good — and that we want nothing to do with them. Because this is something we never want to do, it's always wise to make the move which lets kids back into our orbit. Remember, it's very unlikely that a child will concentrate on school work while in trouble with the boss — even if he or she pretends to. The child's mind is still on the problem, not his or her books. If someone were trying to get you fired, it's unlikely that your lesson plan would have your undivided attention. That's why, when we refuse to settle issues and make things right, our strategic action may prevent us from winning the battle and the war, with ourselves as well as with those we teach.

PART TWENTY-FIVE

THERE ARE EXCEPTIONS TO THE RULE

Strategic Action Rationale: If extenuating circumstances count in a court of law, then they should also count in a classroom.

A few years ago I worked with a teacher who had a problem which may be familiar to many of you. Although she was an excellent teacher, the fact remained that she had two children of her own and periodically had strong feelings of guilt about teaching and not being home with them. Even though her struggle with these guilt feelings did not affect her teaching, the comments of others did much to intensify them. Maybe you are familiar with these thoughtless comments yourself. They come from people who speak before they think. To working mothers their comments range from, "Why do you work?" to "I don't think a woman should work if she has children at home." It's like the question, "When are you going to start your own family?" to the couple who can't, or don't want to, have any children. Unfortunately, none of us can stop these kinds of questions. And neither can we stop the hurt caused by them. We can only learn to live with them, knowing that the majority of the time no hurt was intended. This is what this teacher was doing.

Regardless, I was very much aware of her feelings. On one occasion, knowing that her children were participating in an elementary school program for parents later in the week and that the program was during her conference period, I suggested she might tell her children she would be able to attend. Needless to say, she was thrilled. In her joy, she naturally told a colleague.

A Human Response

The next morning another teacher waited at my door. A busy Saturday schedule, it seemed, would make it very difficult for him to keep an appointment with the dentist. He requested permission to go to the dentist during his conference period the following day. I denied the request.

All the reasons I gave for the denial fell on deaf ears. Concern that he might be late to his next class, or that the dental work might affect his teaching the rest of the day was something I need not worry about, I was assured. Then it came: "I wouldn't have asked — except that you are letting another teacher go. And if she can go, why can't I?'' Good point. But is it?

I tell you this story because situations like this face teachers in the classroom, and administrators in the office, every day of the year. These situations challenge our decisions, our judgment, our fairness, and our relationships with students. The results of these situations can change us too. They can make us resolve to establish absolute rules and operate — always — by the book.

A Deviation From The Norm

Making exceptions to the rule has been a problem that has long plagued teachers and administrators alike. Exceptions get us in a bind, both internally and externally. We all know that policy should be adhered to. There is no doubt about that. Yet, there are also exceptions to the rule — there is no doubt about the reality of this either.

When you consider all points, it's not the exception that's bad. Rather, it's how others — even those you think are not affected — respond to the exception that makes things turn out badly. Somehow, it's just human to think that if someone else gets to do something, then you should get to do something too. What we forget in these rationalizations is that varying circumstances are usually the factor that makes the difference. They are called ''extenuating circumstances.'' It is my personal and professional belief that if extenuating circumstances count in a court of law, then certainly we should give them value in our everyday relationships with students and each other. If we don't, a certain dignity is lost.

The fact remains: Making exceptions should never cause us problems with each other. I worry more about our abandoning exceptions because of the trouble they cause than I do about the problems that result from making them.

Momentarily, students may think making an exception is unfair — but not in the long run. In truth, children are more likely to see the necessity for the exception than are adults — especially if they are taught about the need for considering extenuating circumstances and the need for a teacher to consider them in classroom life. Students have a special feeling about fairness and are touched by it. Allowing a student an extra day on an assignment or allowing a student to take a make-up test may cause others to point their fingers momentarily. But students see and appreciate extenuating circumstances. With the discipline problem, they see allowances made daily. That's why open discussion of this fact — and the reason behind it — can save a teacher considerable time and effort in handling behavior problems. Students need to be told that when teachers do not allow exceptions to the rule, they lose their humanness. The entire class needs to be told that seldom do these exceptions, made in the best interest of the individual student, cause us or anyone else prolonged hurt. Only when we don't make them does lasting harm result.

Like teachers, administrators can always follow the book. Sometimes, they must. Often, the staff will not allow exceptions. If the staff will not permit administrators to consider extenuating circumstances, administrators' hands are often tied in running a school in the same manner that a teacher's are in the classroom.

Summary

There are benefits that come with being able to make an exception, especially in discipline situations. It gives teachers room to operate. It facilitates change and makes it possible for rules to work for us, instead of our working for rules. That's not saying rules are made to be broken. Quite the contrary: Adopting the strategic action of making exceptions to the rules simply makes rules the guideline of their intention, rather than the absolute of their interpretation. Without this attitude, we simply cannot always do what is best for each individual child in a specific situation.

When exceptions are not allowed, human factors of relationships tend to stand still. Worse, people do not get treated individually in a personal way. It's a heavy price to pay just because we cannot allow someone else to get something when we do not. If we intend to resolve discipline problems and teach acceptable behavior, our strategic action must meet human needs with at least as much consideration as we give to our rules.

PART TWENTY-SIX

BEING A HEALER

Strategic Action Rationale: If a teacher does not attempt to be a healer in discipline situations, small problems may become very significant ones.

As teacher, there is one strategic action talent we must all take the time to develop. We need to learn how to be healers. If we don't, little discipline problems can become big ones in a school. Being a healer is using the power of both our responsibility and our intellect to alter difficulty in a positive way for children and others, including ourselves. Being a healer is learning to make any situation better by how we think, what we say, and what we do.

None can deny that such opportunities are presented often in a classroom and in a school. The teacher who is a healer thinks of options and dwells on solutions. The one who is not thinks only of problems and punishments — and maybe even perpetuates problems through action or inaction. If you're not a healer, you may be fanning the flame of unhappiness, whether you intend to or not. That's why adopting this strategic action can do as much for your happiness in education as it can to change unacceptable behavior to acceptable behavior.

A Special Privilege

In the course of a day, a teacher may have more opportunities to heal than a doctor. We occupy a central position in the lives of so many people that we dare not start counting. It isn't only children with whom we deal. Our healing extends to staff, parents, and community. We touch all in more than a casual way. As professional educators, we would be wise to think seriously and happily about this reality.

We aren't just people running a classroom. We are often all things to all people, whether we want it that way or not. Instead of feeling overwhelmed by such a fact, we actually ought to regard this as a real privilege, for it is. What higher honor is there than to be looked to and sought out for help? In truth, a close look will reveal that our biggest professional hurts come when we are not sought out enough. It could be that our strategic attitude, position, and action toward healing are the primary reasons this is so. If we could remember one thing it might alter our behavior toward healing: When anyone looks to us for help — whether it's a student, parent, colleague, or administrator — the person doing the asking is taking a big risk. In truth, the person who seeks our assistance risks his or her whole self. Remember, it is no small thing for the person doing the risking.

Whether we realize it or not, we may increase the risk for those seeking our help. The minute they ask for help they may feel they have caused a still bigger problem by talking to us. Maybe they feel we aren't interested or won't maintain a confidence — or don't want to be involved in their problem. Much depends upon our strategic action. If we regard helping people as a privilege and an honor, the chances are we will seldom make such mistakes. As professional educators, healing is not something we should do. It's something we absolutely must do.

Nothing Elaborate

Contrary to what we might think, healing does not necessarily take huge amounts of time. To catch a child's eye and smile when he or she looks at us often does the trick. Or to ask a student to do something for us that lets the student know we trust his or her ability may be the healing touch. A wink may tell a student all is okay after we have reprimanded behavior. In most cases, we don't have to indulge in elaborate psychic laying on of hands to effect the healing needed in schools today. We just simply need to be warm, friendly, and gentle with the people in our lives.

We need to extend our healing to fellow teachers and administrators as well as students. Our jobs in education are often lonely tasks, for we don't really see our co-workers very much during the school day. Let's also keep in mind that they don't see colleagues either. Sometimes this means that there are those odd moments when our feelings of need for professional association are strong. If our co-workers know that we are the kind of person whose warmth is enfolding, then they, too, can come for a little healing. Again, it's not a matter of being provoked by the length of time it might take from our day. To extend a small gesture toward another human being is not "taking time." It's privileged giving. Where could we be better able to act in our capacity as a healer than with people with whom we work?

And the same goes for parents. Often, they feel isolated from the school. Here again, we have a chance to alleviate pain by a short phone call when we are aware that a child has experienced some anxieties on the school front, and may be presenting them on the home front as well. We must never forget that parents don't know what we know. It's a comfort for them to hear that we are remaining aware, involved, and caring. A phone call, note, or small connection of any kind can be so healing that we can barely emphasize its need enough. That's why healing is a strategic action necessary to keep problems to a minimum as well as to correct ones which have surfaced. Never forget, without a strategic action which includes caring, all our strategic actions may be regarded as manipulations. And people don't like to be manipulated — nor do they like manipulators. Our students are not an exception to those feelings.

Summary

The differences between opportunity and obligation are often in our human perception. In a world where people want so desperately to do something significant and lasting, we have the opportunity to do such things every day. If we see our opportunity to be healers as a privilege, we will make our mark in this world often. If we see these opportunities as a burden, we will miss many chances to do something significant.

If we begin to look at our position as educators from such a point of view, we will see ourselves in a totally new dimension. So will students. Too often, we teach in such a tight frame of "musts" and "have-tos" in regard to our classroom responsibilities that we forget or overlook the possibilities of the larger horizons available to us as professional educators.

Being a healer adds depth and elegance to our teaching discipline. It gives to our teaching that same dimension that the scientist finds when he or she first discovers a solution in the simplest manner and then goes on to implement it in a complete way. We can teach appropriate behavior to our students daily in a routine way that is satisfactory. However, when we regard ourselves in some special way, we have come upon the complete and elegant ingredient. We need only ask, "Is there something more whole we can do than be a healer?" Our answer should help us take advantage of this overwhelmingly rewarding opportunity with all students, including those we call discipline problems. The choice is ours — and so are the rewards once we decide to adopt the strategic action of being a healer.

PART TWENTY-SEVEN

BUYING TIME: A VALUABLE CONTRIBUTION

Strategic Action Rationale: A teacher cannot totally judge the effectiveness of effort. Therefore, if we don't quit on kids, a turnaround at some point in time is possible.

We are tremendously pleased with the progress of many of our students. They are our lifeblood, for it's within their achievement that we find our greatest professional reward. With some kids, however, this is not the case. And our feelings may be quite the opposite. In fact, there are some kids who we feel have wasted their time as well as ours. At certain moments, we may see little value in their being in our class. We may feel that they are a distraction to others who are learning — and to still others who might learn if they were not around.

Sometimes, The Most We Can Do For A Student Is Simply Hang On

As professional educators, we must be honest, of course. However, we must also never, under any circumstances, underestimate our value to young people. And sometimes teacher value and effectiveness cannot be immediately determined. That's why we must realize that all human achievements have beginnings. Too, we must know that there are gaps and plateaus in which progress is not made by all of us. Students are not an exception to this reality.

We've all seen students, whom friends, parents, and police classified as worthless at thirteen, become different people at twenty. And our perspective should tell us that the vast majority of our students become decent, law-abiding, and working citizens in adulthood. We can and should take some credit for these realities.

That's why teachers should think carefully about minimizing their own importance — and especially about quitting on kids. If we just hold on, there may be a turnaround at some point in time. Accepting this professional stance is vitally important. We simply need to buy time with some kids. We need to do so to keep our options open — so that students can keep theirs alive too. Make no mistake, adopting this strategic action is important.

If we keep students in school at times of nonproductivity, we might be doing the single most important thing that can be done for them at that particular time. In truth, we may be doing something more significant than will ever be done for them again. There are a lot of adults who say, "I don't know why they kept me in school, but I sure am grateful that they did." And the penitentiaries are full of people who know that teachers and the school were justified in quitting on them, but who wish they hadn't.

There Are Two Strategic Action Goals Which We Can Adopt To Keep Us From Quitting On Some Students

It's not always easy for a teacher to hang on when students are misbehaving constantly. This is precisely why we need a professional guideline to follow in such cases. And our guideline should contain a different kind of goal: buying time. Our primary goal should be to buy time in a positive way. In these cases, we're just trying to get some kids through the year. This unique goal lets us adopt a strategic action which prevents us from developing the erroneous attitude that we are failing when we are not. We're achieving the only reasonable goal attainable under the circumstances.

Second, our goal should be to buy time so that we might save this student for another teacher. Here, we're not just passing kids along. Quite the contrary, we're keeping their options open, hoping time will alter their attitudes, behavior, and performance. After all, if we choose not to buy time, neither they nor another teacher will have any opportunities. As we take this strategic action course, we need to seek the counsel of fellow teachers, counselors, specialists, and administrators.

In the process of buying time, we need to come to a realization: We cannot presume that school is the only game in town. We can't believe that if some students aren't successful in school, they can't possibly be successful anyplace else. Such is simply not the case. That's why it's vital that while we're buying time, we observe the total development of these students. We can do so by observing their social behavior and emotional, moral, physical, and intellectual successes and failures. When we do, we may discover abilities and interests which allow us to keep doors open that we believed to be closed.

Summary

Without question, we have a responsibility to all students. This includes those who are accepting our teaching and those who are not. In truth, the latter may need us the most. And while we may think we are giving very little to these students, we may be giving them the most necessary element in their lives.

Many of our students who haven't yet found themselves, will. Turnarounds can occur at any time in life. This realization should help us adopt a strategic action of buying time rather than quitting — or feeling failure in a situation in which we have used this action. Though there's little immediate professional satisfaction in this stance, there's more fulfillment in this position than in giving up.

Always keep track of former students — and for good reason. Many who become successful adults were not successful in the classroom. In fact, many successful adults were school failures. Yet, when and if students do find success, we never want it to be said that the school quit on them — or that they made it in spite of school. Rather, we want these kids to say they eventually made it because of us. By adopting the strategic action of buying time while continuing to give help, we will always be able to achieve this goal. After all, we can't win with every student in the present sense. But time can add to our victories.

PART TWENTY-EIGHT

BROAD GENERALIZATIONS ABOUT DISCIPLINE

In closing, I would like to present nineteen broad generalizations about discipline. If you keep these in mind as you handle discipline problems, it can alter your strategic attitude, position, and action.

1. *Never think that, because you are having trouble with a student, he or she is a discipline problem throughout the school.* This assumption may, in many instances, not be true. Often, what is a discipline problem for one teacher may not be for another teacher. Remember this fact every time you encounter a discipline problem. You may be surprised that one or many of your colleagues aren't experiencing any difficulty with your worst discipline problem. Therefore, ask what colleagues are doing — and follow their suggestions. Likewise, realize that there is usually one place, with one teacher, class, or member of the non-certified staff, where appropriate behavior is the norm.

2. *Handling discipline is a personal matter. The student must be treated personally, but a teacher can't take the misbehavior personally.* That's why discipline problems cannot be handled publicly. They must be handled privately. And effective solution requires your professional involvement and expertise rather than your personal reaction.

3. *All discipline problems require time and a willing attitude about giving time.* If you're beating kids out the door at night, don't complain about having continuous discipline problems with the same kids. You will have them. If you are avoiding a relationship with these students rather than building one, neither student attitude nor behavior will change because of teacher action.

4. *Discipline problems are best handled by the individual teacher in his or her classroom.* After all, here is where the problem lies — and here is where the two people who know the full scope of the problem meet. And it is these two people, teacher and student, who must work together again. Until you've had a private conference and given your best effort to resolve the problem, don't send kids to the office. And if you do send students to the office, don't dictate to administrators what they should do. Rather, have administrators utilize their skills and give them room to operate. They can't be put in a position where solving one problem creates another.

5. *We are going to make mistakes in handling students when they misbehave.* When we do, "I'm sorry" can be the first part of our adjustment strategy. Remember, the behavior you present to students is the behavior you'll get from them. If you can't say, "I'm sorry" following a mistake, your students won't be able to say it either.

6. *Many times teacher reaction to student misbehavior multiplies the teacher's problem.* Never forget, you're the professional in the classroom. Therefore, you must always react professionally. To be successful, it's just possible that you'll have to "bite your tongue" to keep from responding to misbehavior in ways that might be regarded by others as worse than the student's misbehavior.

7. *Our attitude about ourselves affects student behavior.* It takes a

mature adult with a good self-concept to handle a roomful of students — as well as the misbehavior which occurs there. If you look down on yourself, on teaching, or on the work of the school, then how you handle discipline problems will be altered. Then, the stage is set for failure rather than success in handling misbehavior.

8. *Student behavior may be a reflection of teacher behavior.* Remember, kids can't respond favorably in problem situations unless you do. Like it or not, this is a reality of living. Therefore, if you're not getting the response you want, check yourself out. You may find that your words are not putting out the fire, but fueling it.

9. *Our failure to keep things in perspective causes discipline problems.* We're teaching in an imperfect world, in an imperfect school, in an imperfect classroom, to imperfect students. And we are imperfect, too. Therefore, imperfection, not perfection, is the condition in a school. Sometimes, it's forgetting this reality that gives both our approach and our action in discipline situations little chance for success from the beginning.

10. *Never forget, children with problems at school usually have more severe problems at home.* That's why home and school must work together. These children need our help and we need theirs. Remember, all is not well for the child having problems at school. Therefore, when you have a problem, call parents. And don't wait — or a bigger problem may result before cooperative efforts can begin.

11. Always keep one thing in mind when handling discipline problems. It'll help your balance, perspective, peace of mind, and actions if you do. *Students with discipline problems often dislike themselves and are usually disliked by other students.* Remember, people who do not behave appropriately do not lead happy lives. And everyone has to have someone in order to enjoy the fruits of living. These kids need you. With you, they can change. Without you, more inappropriate behavior is the probability.

12. *Keep in mind that all teacher discipline must promote student self-discipline.* If it doesn't, we can only expect to work on the same problems with the same students every day. Therefore, slow down. Then, spend as much time with persuasive teaching as you do with strict enforcement and you'll find kids responding in positive and constructive ways.

13. As you approach a discipline problem, keep one probability in mind. *Students with discipline problems have few, if any, meaningful conversations or relationships with any adults.* You must change this reality to change behavior. Therefore, if you assume the role of boss or immovable authority, or an uncaring stance, you may widen the gap. Remember, these kids *don't know how* to deal with an adult relationship because they don't have any. Unless you take them in, therefore, you unintentionally shut them out.

14. *Whether we like it or not, children regarded as discipline problems are "rejected" by the adult world.* If we want to change their behavior in the classroom, changing this reality is a first step. Remember, inclusion rather than exclusion is a necessity to change inappropriate behavior to appropriate behavior. You cannot reject students and change their behavior no matter how you feel. If you do, they'll fight you whether they win the battle or not.

15. *Students having adjustment problems usually have a large void in their personal lives.* Usually this void is other people. Herein lies your power and effectiveness in changing inappropriate behavior to appropriate behavior. Humans are social beings. We are not loners. Until you can get students who are discipline problems involved with others, you can't get them to accept responsibility toward others.

16. *How a teacher handles an individual problem does affect that teacher's relationship with all of his or her students.* Remember, the class watches — and makes judgments — regarding how you handle misbehaving students. And other students can identify with classmates when they're in trouble. They can imagine you treating them as you are treating their classmates. Therefore, don't let your handling of discipline problems destroy your relationship with other students.

17. Regardless of your feelings, the human condition seems to reflect, "If you like me, I like you." It also reflects, "If you don't like me, I don't like you." *Therefore, if a child believes that a teacher likes him or her, the child will act differently, but maybe only toward that one teacher.* Remember this fact and you may begin to change the behavior of your worst discipline problem.

18. Make no mistake. *Teachers who are approachable have fewer discipline problems.* Remember, if you look down on problems, you automatically look down on the people who have them. Too, an open door policy does not mean you are approachable. Lots of teachers talk about their "door always being open" — until someone comes in.

19. *Generally speaking, people act as they think you think they will act.* That's why high expectations are a requirement for changing behavior. Never forget this truth of learning. It applies to learning appropriate behavior. If you lower your expectations for some kids, you'll probably get the behavior you expect.

This is the first of two books on discipline published by The Master Teacher. *Before You Can Discipline ... Vital Professional Foundations for Classroom Management* has dealt with student needs and three teacher strategies: attitude, position, and action. The second book, *You Can Handle Them All — A Discipline Model for Handling Over One Hundred*

Different Misbehaviors at Home and at School, deals with handling students, such as the talker, defier, hater, class clown, cheater, and liar, who exhibit specific behaviors. It defines and tells how to correct more than one hundred misbehaviors we deal with constantly in the classroom, counselor's office, and principal's office. In this book, each student misbehavior is broken down into four parts: (1) precise behavior, (2) effects on class and teacher, (3) recommended action, and (4) mistakes commonly made by teachers, counselors, and administrators. The book was written in outline form so that it can be used as a desk reference book for teachers, counselors, and administrators. I hope you will avail yourself of this book, too.

Before You Can Discipline ... Vital Professional Foundations for Classroom Management has dealt with foundations. And the foundations presented in this book are vital to your effectiveness as an educator in handling discipline problems. In fact, if you make these foundations a part of your being, I promise you that you will come quickly to know how important you are to young people — and find more happiness and satisfaction in teaching as a result.